I0163751

Write For You

The CGW Guide to Publishing

"Everyone has a book inside them"

But how did it get there?

And more importantly, how do you get it out?

Christopher Greenaway

&

Amelia Hartley

CGW
PUBLISHING

2010

Write For You

The CGW Guide to Publishing

First Edition: October 2010

ISBN 978-0-9565358-3-2

'CGW', 'CG Writing' and 'CGW Publishing' are trading names of Revelation Consulting Limited. Registered in England and Wales, number 6984624. Registered office: 106 Park Road, Rugby, Warwickshire, CV21 2QX, UK.

Published by:

CGW Publishing
B 1502
PO Box 15113
Birmingham
B2 2NJ
United Kingdom

www.cgwpublishing.com

mail@cgwpublishing.com

Contents

Why Publish a Book?

A book is something sacred and special.

Tens of thousands of years ago, only priests and royalty had access to the written word, in Sanskrit, Hieroglyphics, Cuneiform, papyrus scrolls, even cave paintings. Knowledge could be passed from generation to generation, but only by the select few who were taught the written word.

Perhaps you can remember the pleasure of being read to as a child, or you can remember your favourite childhood story books. Perhaps you can remember learning to read and write at school. It's easy to think that every child today has the opportunity to learn this basic skill, and according to UNESCO, 81% of the world's population is literate, yet in some countries, only 25% of the population can read and write. It is something that anyone can learn, but it is not an automatic privilege.

In developed countries such as the UK, USA, Australia and most of Europe, 99% of the population is literate. To put this in perspective, one or two of the other children in your year at school could not read and write. In the UK, with a population of around 60 Million, that means that 600,000 people cannot read and write. That's more than the entire population of the British county of Cornwall.

The advent of the printing press made books available to more people, and the evolution of technology, from lithographic presses through to today's digital printers, has made books more and more readily accessible for a wider audience.

Even so, the roots of books, in our history and in our own lives, make a book something precious and valuable, and to write a book confers a status and credibility that is unparalleled.

A book has to have its own worth and must stand on its own merit. To write and publish a book, it has to be good enough for someone to want to read it. Just to have a book confers a superficial level of credibility, but only a good book will receive the praise from its readers that leads to word of mouth sales and a true following for the book and its author.

If you want to express the book that is inside you, waiting to get out, then a good publisher will help you to shape your ideas and create something that you will be proud of and your readers will love.

As an author, your words connect you with your readers through space and time. Even though they may share in your ideas, many thousands of miles away and years in the future, that connection is very much in the here and now.

People have their favourite books and favourite authors. Every serious Sunday newspaper has a literature section. Annual literature festivals and high profile prizes recognise the contribution made by authors to our heritage and to our civilisation.

And all of this together means that, as an author, you will become part of that heritage and pass your valuable life experiences on to new generations.

From Author to Reader

Although it's often said that everyone has a book in them, not everyone finds it easy to articulate their idea or their passion. Some people have a story to tell, others have a hobby or interest that they want to share. Some people want to capture their professional expertise and then use their book to add credibility to their business ventures.

If you have spent time, running your idea around in your mind or even capturing it purely for your own pleasure, the first step is to put pen to paper or, ideally, fingers to keyboard.

Some people sit down to write a book. Others sit down to capture their ideas and don't plan for the end result to be a book. It doesn't matter what motivates you to begin, the important thing is that you begin somehow.

As you write your book, you are entering a chain of events that leads from you to your reader, through a network of publishers, retailers and other companies who get your work into the hands of your readers.

When an author writes a book, the finished text is called a manuscript. It's a relatively plain text document which may or may not contain illustrations and formatting and which can't be turned directly into a printed book.

The author then has two ways to get their book into print; either self-publish or find a publisher to help.

In reality, self publishing simply means that the author also acts as a publisher, so whatever route the author chooses, in order to sell their book, they have to publish it.

A publisher is simply a company or facility that turns the author's original manuscript into a printed book and then makes that book, or title as it is known in the book industry, available for sale.

A publisher will agree to print the author's book and then liaise with printers and retailers, sometimes making changes that will help to sell the book such as cover design or editing.

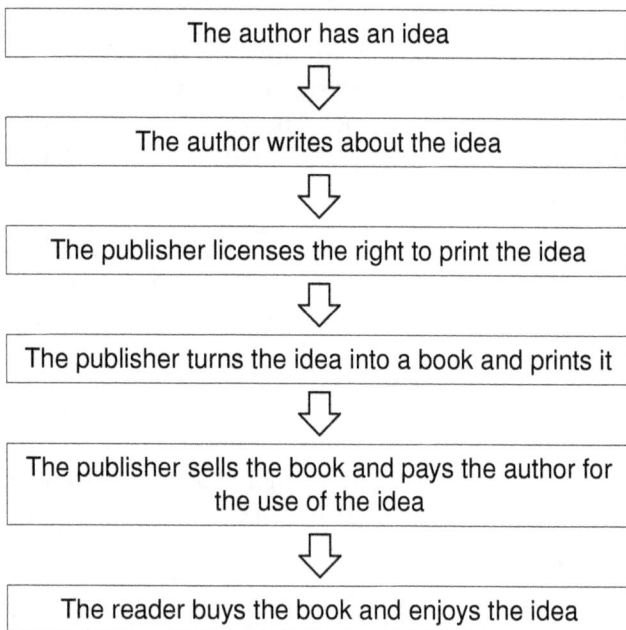

The author has an idea

⇩

The author writes about the idea

⇩

The publisher licenses the right to print the idea

⇩

The publisher turns the idea into a book and prints it

⇩

The publisher sells the book and pays the author for the use of the idea

⇩

The reader buys the book and enjoys the idea

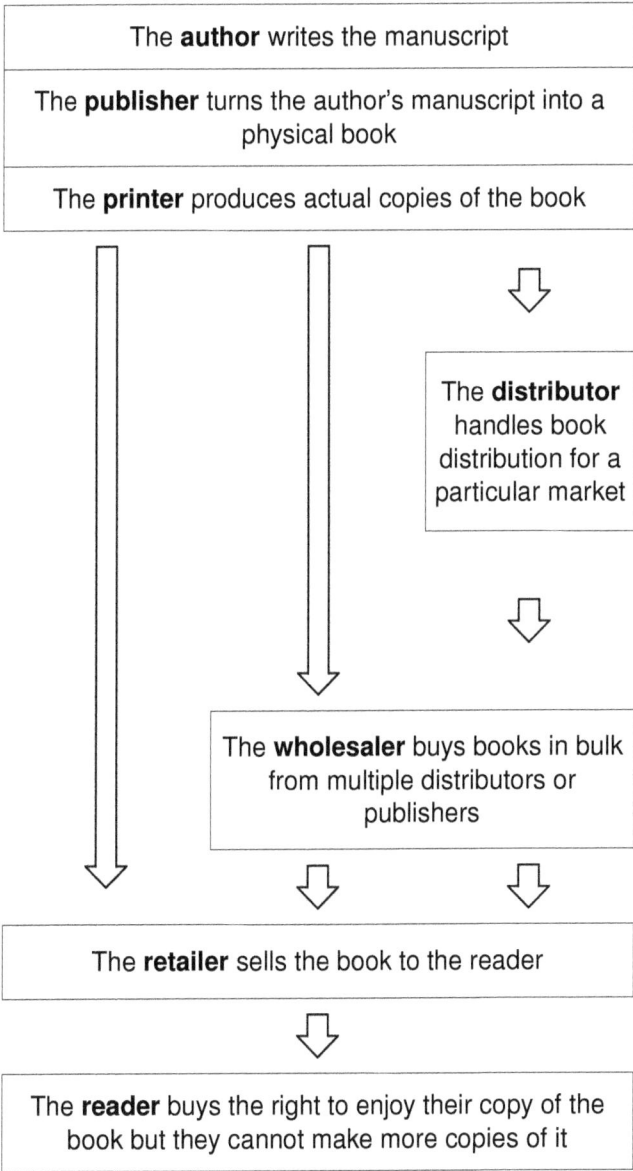

The **author** writes the manuscript

The **publisher** turns the author's manuscript into a physical book

The **printer** produces actual copies of the book

The **distributor** handles book distribution for a particular market

The **wholesaler** buys books in bulk from multiple distributors or publishers

The **retailer** sells the book to the reader

The **reader** buys the right to enjoy their copy of the book but they cannot make more copies of it

A distributor specialises in large volume wholesale of books for particular markets, typically geographic. As far as book sales are concerned, the world is divided into regions and different publishers can have different rights for those regions. For example, an author can sign a contract with one publisher for Europe and a different one for the USA.

In reality, some of these companies specialise in just one of these functions, whereas others combine a number of functions.

For example:

- Coutts is a wholesaler, supplying books to the academic and scientific markets.

- Amazon combines wholesale and retail because they generally buy direct from the publisher.

- Gardners Books/CPC combine printing, distribution and wholesale.

- Lulu combines publishing, printing and retail.

- CGW Publishing is an independent publisher that specialises in supporting authors who run service businesses.

The international book ordering process

The global book market relies on the ISBN number – the International System for Book Numbering.

A book doesn't have to have an ISBN number, but without one it cannot easily be ordered by book shops and the author would have to sell it direct to any retailer, which is so time consuming that it is unlikely to be profitable.

An electronic ordering system, administered by a company in the UK called Nielsen, allows any book retailer, anywhere in the world to place an order for a book and have that book sent from the publisher or wholesaler to the retailer for sale to the customer.

ISBN numbers are now aligned with Universal Product Codes (UPC), used to identify consumer products. Each country has its own prefix number, and all books originate from a fictional country called 'Bookland', therefore you will often hear an ISBN number referred to as a 'Bookland EAN' (European Article Number).

ISBN numbers are 13 digits long, in the following format. This is called an ISBN-13.

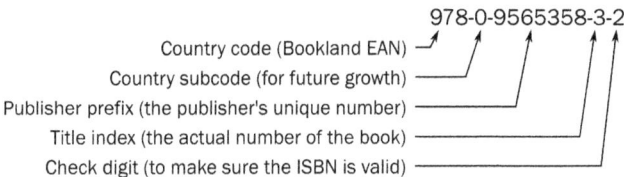

978-0-9565358-3-2

Country code (Bookland EAN)
Country subcode (for future growth)
Publisher prefix (the publisher's unique number)
Title index (the actual number of the book)
Check digit (to make sure the ISBN is valid)

ISBN numbers used to be 10 digits long until the advent of print on demand publishing which led to ISBN numbers being allocated much more quickly.

An old ISBN-10 number would look like this:

0-956-53583-6

The last digit is different than for an ISBN-13 because it is a check digit, used to make sure that the rest of the ISBN number is valid.

The ISBN system was expanded into the UPC system and an extra country subcode was added to double capacity. Currently, ISBN numbers begin with 978-0, and when the second country subcode is used, you will see ISBN numbers beginning with 978-1.

On the back cover of a book, the ISBN number would look like this:

9 780956 535832

Every ISBN number on the database has a record associated with it which contains information such as the publisher, price and distributor as well as information about the book and author.

Book shops have access to this database and when a customer wants to order a particular book, they can look up the book's data record and see where to order it from – direct from the publisher, or from a wholesaler or distributor.

The order for the book goes this way:

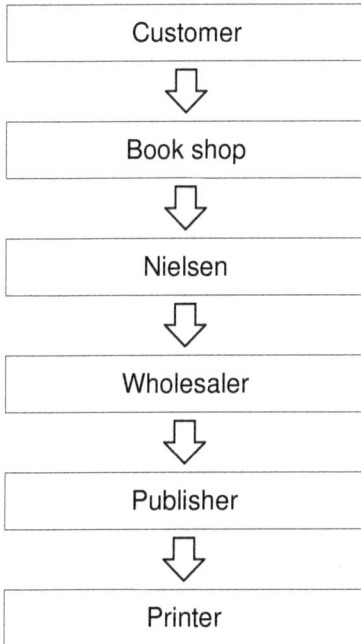

```
┌─────────────────────────────────┐
│            Customer             │
└─────────────────────────────────┘
                ⇩
┌─────────────────────────────────┐
│            Book shop            │
└─────────────────────────────────┘
                ⇩
┌─────────────────────────────────┐
│             Nielsen             │
└─────────────────────────────────┘
                ⇩
┌─────────────────────────────────┐
│            Wholesaler           │
└─────────────────────────────────┘
                ⇩
┌─────────────────────────────────┐
│            Publisher            │
└─────────────────────────────────┘
                ⇩
┌─────────────────────────────────┐
│             Printer             │
└─────────────────────────────────┘
```

The book shop then places an order and waits for the book to arrive. The ISBN database manager passes that order to the relevant supplier who might be a publisher, distributor or wholesaler, and that supplier then sends the book along with an invoice for payment to the retailer.

The customer pays the retailer for the book and the retailer pays the supplier, who pays the publisher, who pays the author.

The physical copy of the book goes this way:

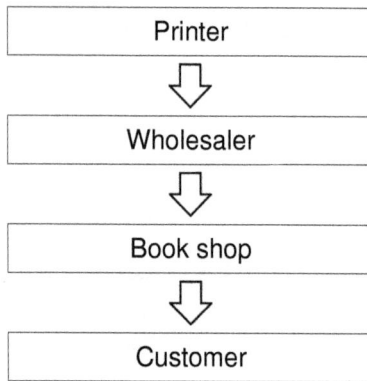

```
┌─────────────────────────────┐
│           Printer           │
└─────────────────────────────┘
              ⇩
┌─────────────────────────────┐
│          Wholesaler         │
└─────────────────────────────┘
              ⇩
┌─────────────────────────────┐
│          Book shop          │
└─────────────────────────────┘
              ⇩
┌─────────────────────────────┐
│           Customer          │
└─────────────────────────────┘
```

Finally, the payment for the book goes this way:

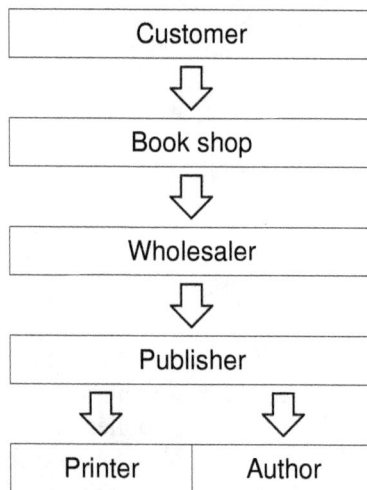

```
┌─────────────────────────────┐
│           Customer          │
└─────────────────────────────┘
              ⇩
┌─────────────────────────────┐
│          Book shop          │
└─────────────────────────────┘
              ⇩
┌─────────────────────────────┐
│          Wholesaler         │
└─────────────────────────────┘
              ⇩
┌─────────────────────────────┐
│          Publisher          │
└─────────────────────────────┘
        ⇩             ⇩
┌──────────────┬──────────────┐
│    Printer   │    Author    │
└──────────────┴──────────────┘
```

The publisher pays the printer for the production of the physical book and the author for the creative content of the book.

Routes to Publishing

The role of a publisher is to take the author's manuscript, the raw expression of their idea, and turn it into a physical book that can be sold in book shops.

There are different types of publishers, specialising in different types of book or different markets.

Lists of publishers are available on the Internet, or you can buy a book called The Writers' and Artists' Yearbook which contains publishing, press and media contacts as well as advice for authors.

Traditional publishers

We've heard it said that the publishing industry causes a lot of disappointment. Certainly, what makes a story or idea interesting to the author does not always make it popular with readers.

Traditionally, publishers are highly risk averse because of the production costs of a book. However, print on demand has turned this on its head, although the attitude of the major publishing houses has not changed significantly, because the printing costs are now only a small part of their cost of sale.

Before the advent of digital printing, it was only cost effective to produce books in quantities of tens of thousands. If you look at the 'title page verso' of a book (the page with all the publishing information on it), you will see a list of dates, for example:

First Edition: June 1986
Reprinted: August 1988
Second Edition: January 1991

This means that the first print run in June 1986 produced enough copies to last for two years of sales, and the book was printed again in August 1988. The book was then reissued with some corrections and additions in January 1991 and hasn't been printed again since then.

A publisher doesn't want to print 30,000 copies of a book, only to have them take up valuable space in a warehouse. They'll sell books at a fraction of their cover price rather than hold them in stock, especially as seasonal titles or books by current minor celebrities have a very short shelf life.

The traditional publishing model is based on the author selling the book. They will publish just about anything that has a popular celebrity's name on it, and for minor celebrities, they expect book signings, radio and TV interviews, newspaper syndication and so on. For the majority of authors, they expect the author to put forward a business case for the book which guarantees sales.

Traditional publishers raise a barrier to entry for authors because their focus is purely on book sales.

The problem for most business authors is that book sales are not the primary way that they generate profits. Of course, many authors would love to sit back and live off book royalties, but this is not realistic for anyone who has not spent a lifetime working hard at developing their own personal brand. In order to generate ongoing book sales, the author has to keep on building their brand, which means the author has to keep on working.

Business books simply don't sell in anywhere near the volumes of popular fiction, so a business author generally has to see the book as part of an overall business strategy, not a business in itself. This isn't a comment on the quality of business books, only a fact that business books appeal to a more narrow audience than popular fiction.

Vanity Publishers

'Vanity publishers' are publishers who will take any book and put it into print for you for a very large fee. They appeal to people who just want to have a copy of their own book on their coffee table, hence the name. They apply almost no quality or acceptance criteria to books that they accept because they do not need to assess the profitability of a book.

Print on demand has all but put vanity publishers out of business, because anyone can see their book in print without having to pay the high set up costs charged by a vanity publisher.

Agents

An agent is someone who represents the author, allowing the author to concentrate on writing while the agent arranges and negotiates contracts, arranges marketing, publicity and other important activities.

Some agents work for a fixed fee but generally they would expect to sign a representation contract with an author for which they get paid a percentage of royalties.

Some authors think that without an agent, they won't get a publishing contract. While an agent knows how to write a book proposal and can send it to the right people, they can't guarantee securing a contract. A good agent will provide objective feedback to the author to increase their chances of getting a contract. A poor agent will take a fee for proposing the book to publishers whether they believe the book will sell or not.

A good test is to speak to a number of agents and if one or more are prepared to take the book on a commission basis, that probably means that they think it's good enough to secure a contract in which case you can approach publishers direct.

Self Publishing

If you don't plan to publish many books then you can use self publishing services such as CreateSpace or Lulu, which is a service that sits in front of a printing company called Lightning Source. Lulu offers basic formatting, ready-made cover designs and ISBN number allocation, as well as an online book shop.

Some services charge a set up cost, others offer free set up but hide inflated printing and distribution costs, recouping their set up costs from book sales.

Self publishing means that anyone can publish a book with no critical assessment, but in reality their book doesn't reach a significant readership through book shops, so themselves critical review process takes place at the point of sale rather than at the point of writing, editing or publishing.

If you are considering self publishing, it is important to at least have someone else proof read and edit the book, as it is very easy to overlook mistakes when you've been staring at text on a computer screen for hours.

Self publishing removes all barriers to entry, apart from money, so there are no quality controls or checks on books entering the market. This can leave readers with the perception that all self published books are of poor quality.

Having a publisher means that your book has been evaluated and edited to be of publishable quality, and that gives your book credibility.

Independent Publishers

There are a growing number of independent publishers who specialise in particular market areas. They are not tied to any of the mainstream publishing, printing or distribution channels and they can support authors in ways that the major publishing houses do not.

Many authors dream that their book will be 'picked up' by a major publisher and will appear on the best sellers list, just as many musicians dream of signing a contract with a major recording label.

The reality is that the traditional publishers are extremely risk averse and will only offer a publishing contract when they are certain that a book will sell in high volumes. If the book enables the author to make money in other ways, for example from training, consulting or public speaking, traditional publishers are not interested as that does not lead to profit for them.

Independent publishers can give an author more creative and marketing control over their books, and can offer a more personalised service which is valuable where the author wants to publish as part of a greater business strategy.

Also, by using print on demand services, an independent publisher can release new editions of a book much more frequently than a traditional publisher can, so the author can incorporate new ideas and corrections much more easily.

When a traditional publisher buys the rights to publish a book, they are also taking control of the creative and marketing aspects of the book. The publisher will typically design the cover, decide when and how the book is launched, control the way the book is marketed and so on.

This can mean that a publisher buys the rights to a book and doesn't actually put it into print because they want to launch another book first which competes for market share. If the author has signed an exclusive contract, they have no control over this.

With an independent publisher, the author should expect to have more creative input and more control over the way that their book is marketed, so the contract represents more of a collaborative partnership between author and publisher.

Of course, publishing is a business, so both the publisher and author will be working together to generate profits from book sales. The author brings their creativity and the publisher brings their production and marketing expertise and each benefits from this mutual partnership.

Print on Demand

Today, a book goes straight from computer to printed copy with no manual intervention, thanks to a service called 'print on demand'.

Years ago, if you wanted to print a leaflet describing your services, you would have a printer produce them in a large enough quantity to make the printing cost effective. They would make special printing plates, like the ones used in newspaper presses, that were so costly to produce that you would need to order many thousands of leaflets to make it cost effective. This method of printing is called 'litho' or 'offset' and it is still in use today for newspapers, business stationery and anything that is printed in the tens of thousands of copies.

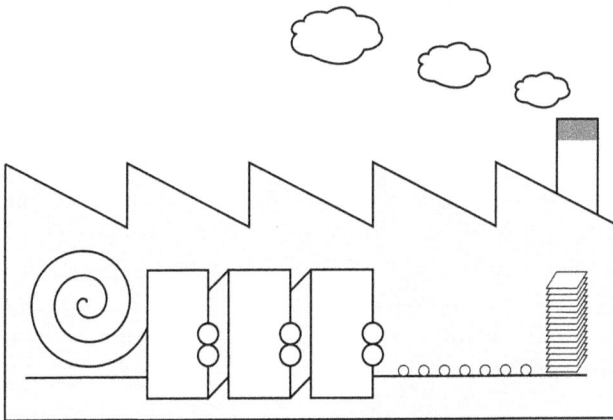

Today, you keep a file on your computer, and when you want to send someone a leaflet, you print it at home. The cost for one copy is higher than the cost for one copy printed on an 'offset' press, but since you'll never send out more than a few dozen, the overall cost is a fraction of what you would have paid for 10,000 leaflets.

As the technology improves, the quality of a home inkjet printer gets closer to the quality of 'offset' printing, although the cost will never compare for large quantities.

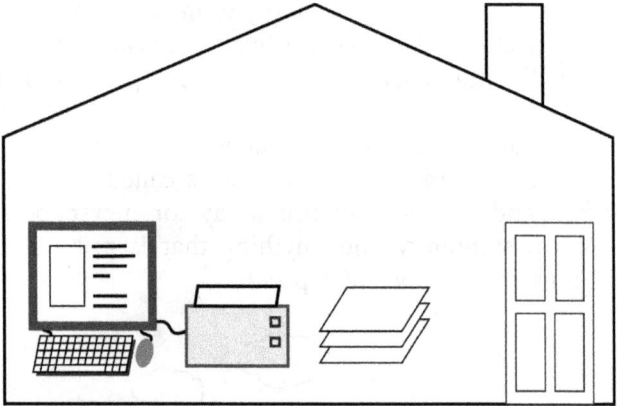

A compromise between the two is the modern digital press. It's a professional version of the printer you have at home or in the office and it makes small print runs of up to a few thousand copies cost effective for items such as leaflets, business cards and training manuals. When you need to order some more copies, you just call the printer, they look up your file and click 'print'.

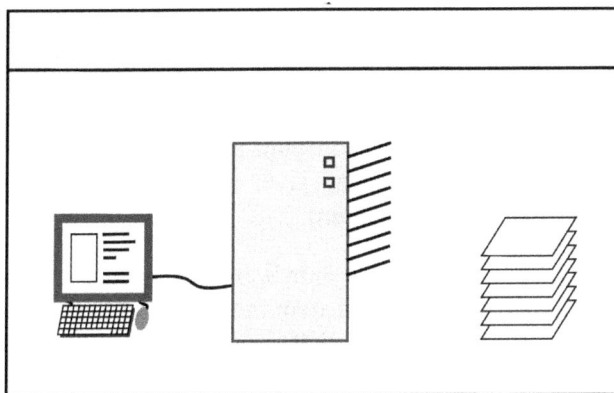

Specialist 'print on demand' book printers simply take this concept a step further. A paperback or hardback book is a more complex product than a business card, so they have special digital presses that produce the book, cut it to size and bind it.

The final result is almost indistinguishable from one produced on an 'offset' press.

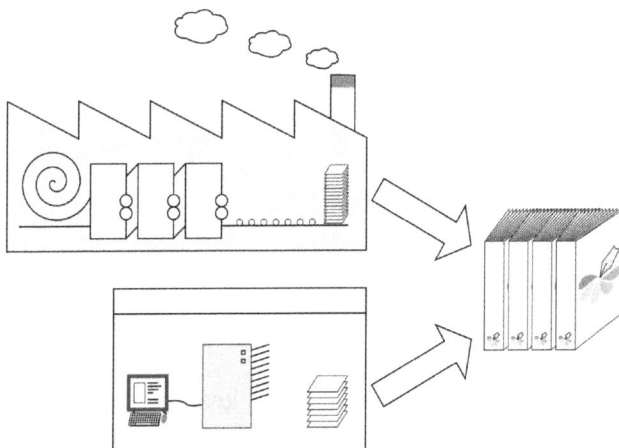

'Offset' printing requires large print runs to be cost effective. With print on demand, the cost per copy is the same regardless of the number of copies printed.

On the other hand, if you plan to sell 10,000 copies of a book, offset printing gives a far lower cost per copy than print on demand.

If you want to produce your book in a format that is not a standard print on demand format then either offset or high volume digital printing are the only options.

Whilst the low production cost per copy of offset printing might seem tempting, you have to think about where you're going to put 10,000 books. That's quite a lot of boxes. If you placed 10,000 copies of a typical paperback novel in one big pile, it would be 280 metres high.

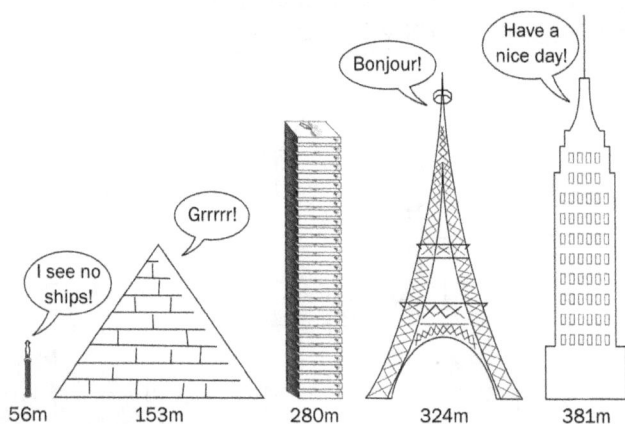

| 56m | 153m | 280m | 324m | 381m |

10,000 books is a lot of boxes to keep in your garage, and that's why wholesalers get a percentage of the revenue from a book.

The book that you are reading now is produced using the print on demand process. The printer achieves economy of scale by printing books in high volumes, and the digital printing process means that each book that comes out of the printing press can be different.

Let's say that both a traditional offset printer and a print on demand printer both print 1,000 books in a day.

With an offset printer, all 1,000 books are the same.

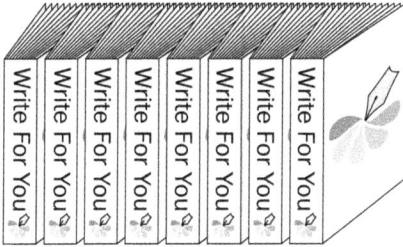

With print on demand, each of the 1,000 can be a different book. You and 999 other authors can share the production costs.

The only real disadvantage of print on demand is that the appearance of your book is limited to the formats that are used by the print on demand supplier. Whilst the book sizes and paper types are not a restriction, if you want your cover to be unusual or decorative, you will need to use a high volume printing process which increases the number of books that need to be produced for the process to be cost effective. While the cost per copy will be acceptable, you need to invest in a large stock of books, and you need somewhere to keep them.

One way to solve the problem of book storage is to set up a distribution arrangement with a distributor who can hold your books in their warehouse. However, the charges for this can be quite high.

Both volume and POD printers produce books in high volumes to keep the unit cost as low as possible.

There are two main reasons for using a print on demand service.

Firstly, it means that a book never goes out of print. Years ago, when publishers printed a book only to find that it didn't sell, they disposed of surplus copies through book clubs and discount book shops. When a book no longer sold in sufficient volumes to warrant an 'offset' print run, it was removed from circulation altogether.

Today, there is next to no cost to the publisher in keeping a file on a computer, so a book can remain 'in print' forever.

Secondly, print on demand lowers barriers to entry to the market for new authors.

Because the risk is reduced, the publisher has to be less concerned about return on investment and can support titles and authors which are not guaranteed best sellers, while the author can use the book to leverage other revenue streams such as consultancy, training and public speaking.

With print on demand (POD), a book is generally not held on a shelf in either a warehouse or book shop.

First, the book must be set up for printing, with the following sequence of events taking place:

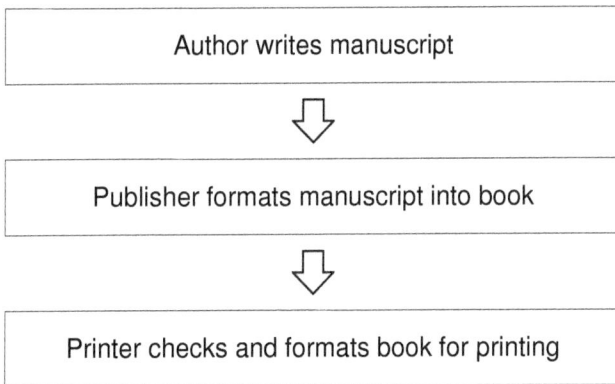

```
┌─────────────────────────────────────────────┐
│           Author writes manuscript            │
└─────────────────────────────────────────────┘
                     ⇩
┌─────────────────────────────────────────────┐
│      Publisher formats manuscript into book   │
└─────────────────────────────────────────────┘
                     ⇩
┌─────────────────────────────────────────────┐
│    Printer checks and formats book for printing│
└─────────────────────────────────────────────┘
```

This set up process normally takes a week or two, and the publisher would normally get a proof copy to check for any mistakes and printing errors.

It's much easier to correct any errors at this stage, because no matter how much you look at the book on a computer screen, it can be very different in print. The legibility of diagrams, the clarity of text and the cover design can look very different on screen compared to the finished product.

Therefore, up to a month should be allowed for this part of the process.

When someone orders a copy of the book, these events take place, normally within 2 to 5 days:

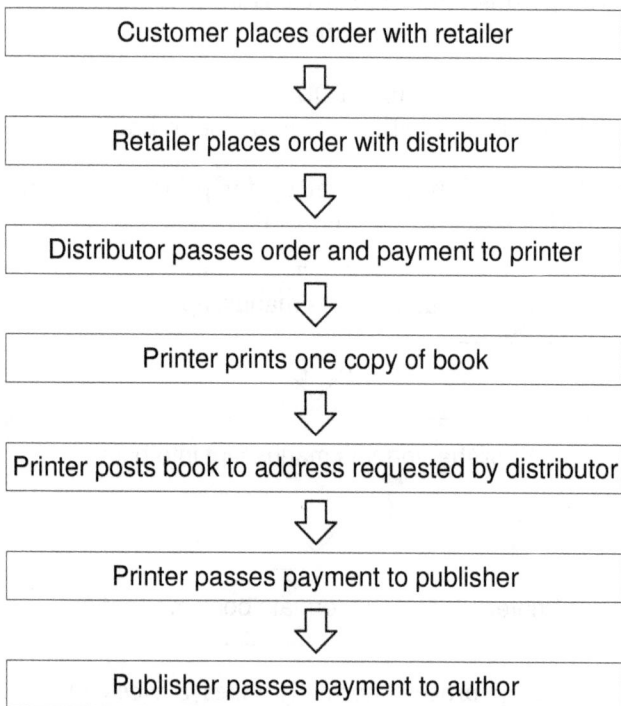

Customer places order with retailer

⇩

Retailer places order with distributor

⇩

Distributor passes order and payment to printer

⇩

Printer prints one copy of book

⇩

Printer posts book to address requested by distributor

⇩

Printer passes payment to publisher

⇩

Publisher passes payment to author

The distributor can be the publisher, the printer or the wholesaler, depending on the different services offered by these companies.

Sometimes, the only way to produce a book is to print it in volume, perhaps because of the format restrictions of the POD printing process.

It's also possible to launch a new book using POD and then move to a traditional printing process when sales volumes would make that cost effective.

Book Production

Walk into any book shop and you will see that books come in many different shapes and sizes. Open them up and you'll see just as wide a variety of formats, fonts, papers and illustrations.

Publishers try to make books look more appealing on the shelf, and they try to make them stand out from other books.

Ultimately, the book has to be easy to read, because that will keep the reader engaged longer than fancy fonts and gimmicky graphics.

There are many factors to consider when designing and producing a book, so it's definitely worth spending some time looking at other books and deciding what you think fits your subject matter and personality.

Organising Your Book

Whatever the subject of your book, think about the journey that you want to take your readers through.

If your book is a story, your story will lead your reader through an emotional journey.

If your book is a business book, the content might lead the reader through a process, such as a sales process or the journey to developing leadership skills.

If your book is a collection of poetry, think about organising the poems around a theme so that they lead the reader through an interesting journey such as a life story or the changing seasons.

Making a Start

Many writers worry about 'writer's block' which is generally a sign that they don't know how to put their ideas into words. Yet they probably find that they can describe the subject to a friend or colleague quite easily.

If you have suffered from writer's block then the problem is very simple – you are most likely trying to write in the style you think is 'best' rather than writing in your own style. Write as if you are having a conversation with an imaginary reader and just let the words come out.

If you worry that your own words or style don't sound 'formal' or 'business-like' or 'credible' then don't worry, because your readers want to connect with you, not with a news reader. Your book conveys your personality, and when you try to take that out, the book loses the very quality that makes the reader want to read it. The book can become dry and lifeless and, ultimately, unreadable.

Don't worry about getting the words exactly right at the beginning – that's what editing is for. Writing is about getting your words out in a rough draft, and getting as much out as you can.

Some writers, particularly when writing fiction, like to start at the beginning and work all the way through to the end. Non-fiction books are usually different in that their 'story' is not a single thread through time, so you can write in layers, going back and adding more into each chapter as you work through your ideas. Therefore, getting the overall structure in place first is important.

Think about the message that you want to get across and imagine taking a reader on a journey. If you are writing non-fiction, that journey is about learning and understanding. If your book is fiction or poetry, that journey is an emotional one which echoes the subject of the book.

There are many different ways to organise your book, and the most important thing for you to remember is that the structure must make sense to the reader so that the book is easy to read and follow along with. Your readers will turn your words back into images, sounds, tastes, smells and feelings and anything that interrupts that in your writing style will make the book more tiring to read. When people say that they "can't put a book down", that's more likely to be because it's easy and engaging to read than because the subject matter is particularly relevant to them.

Book Formats

Different printers are able to produce books in different formats or sizes, however there are a number of book sizes which are more commonly used. Some authors and publishers try to make their books stand out by using non-standard formats, and while this may attract initial interest, it is still the content of the book that leads to long term success.

In general, business books are printed in 5" x 8" or 6" x 9" format, popular fiction is smaller and academic text books and cartoon books are larger.

When you're thinking about the actual appearance of your book, have a look at your own book shelf or go to a local book shop. Find some books that you like and see what format they're in. Regardless of what you think your readers might like or what is the 'right' format, start with the format that you like because that is part of your book's personality.

Your book can look however you want, so the only design consideration is cost. The more that the appearance of your book deviates from the print on demand standard, the higher the production cost per book.

Book Length

As with format, take a look at some books that you like and see how many pages they have. As a rough guide, the number of words on a printed page are as follows:

Size	Words per page	
	Text only:	With illustrations:
5" x 8"	200	150
6" x 9"	300	250
A4	400	350

A typical business book can be between 40,000 and 60,000 words long. Fiction books might be up to 150,000 words long or even more. This book is just under 25,000 words long.

Books with numerous illustrations or books containing poetry with one poem per page can of course be much shorter in word count for the same number of pages.

The shortest book that can be printed using the print on demand method is 80 pages, because of the binding process. This means that your book needs to be at least 16,000 words long, or about 12,000 words if you have illustrations like the ones in this book.

If you want to write a book that is shorter than about 16,000 words then a printing company will be able to produce a 'short run' and bind then manually for you. The cost per copy will be relatively high, though.

If you find that you haven't written enough words to reach the minimum page count then you could consider using an editing or ghost writing service.

An editor can give you advice on areas that you can expand on, and a ghost writer can do the actual writing work for you while you retain complete credit as the book's author.

There are no rules for the length of a book. If you write fiction, you might consider publishing a collection of short stories rather than a single novel.

If you are writing a non-fiction book, you could add case studies, practical guidance for the reader or have some information about your company and its services. It's a good idea to keep anything like that separate to the main text, otherwise the book could be interpreted as an advert rather than as neutral and informative.

Language

There are many different writing styles that you can adopt. Once you have chosen one that is right for you, stick to it throughout your book unless you have a specific reason to change and you can mark out the reasons for that so that it makes sense to the reader.

One of the most common variations in style is between active and passive voice, and this is particularly relevant to non-fiction books.

Active voice is a conversational style where I am speaking directly to you about the subject.

Passive voice is a formal style where the author speaks to the reader indirectly about the subject.

Passive voice is often used in business communications and hence business books. It is more neutral, but is also more tiring to read.

Active voice, or writing in the first person, is easy to read because it sounds like a face to face conversation. You can connect with your readers more easily and more personally, but it's not every author's preference.

Above all else, write so that your personality comes through.

Fonts

There are lots of fonts on your computer for you to choose from, but fonts do not work in the same way on screen as they do in print. Therefore, it's worth understanding a few technical details about fonts so that your book will look its best when printed.

'Print fonts' are specifically designed to be easy to read when printed onto white paper. As a print font gets bigger, its appearance changes from this:

AaBbCcDdEe

To this:

AaBbCcDdEe

The clarity remains the same because the font is created as a set of lines and curves. No matter what the size, the font always appears clear and smooth.

A screen creates images differently than a printer does, so a screen font looks like this when printed:

AaBbCcDdEe

AaBbCcDdEe

And like this on screen:

AaBbCcDdEe

AaBbCcDdEe

As you can see, a screen can't display fonts in the same way that a printer can. Where the printer can create smooth curves, the screen has to simulate smooth curves with shades of grey:

Because of this limitation, screen fonts are designed to avoid complex curves with the result that the font looks better on screen but worse in print.

The thing to remember is that, just because a font looks good on screen, it isn't necessarily readable in print. One of the biggest problems is using decorative fonts which are fine for chapter titles but not for the main text. Anything which is tiring to read will put the reader off, no matter how good the content is.

Fonts are also designed to be used at particular sizes which improve their readability.

A commonly used screen font is Verdana, and because it is the font used for most web pages, some people use it for printed text too.

When you are deciding how you want your book to appear, print out pages of text in different fonts and give them to other people to read.

Printers recommend 'serif' fonts such as Garamond at a size of 13 points. Alternatives include Times New Roman, Book Antiqua and Palatino.

A serif font has decorative elements at the ends of lines within the characters, like this:

ABCDEF

The alternative is a 'sans serif' font, where the characters are simple lines with no decoration:

ABCDEF

Generally, serif fonts are used in print because the extra elements improve the font's legibility when used on paper. However, they make the text more difficult to display on screen, so sans serif fonts are more often used on web pages.

You can find some examples to compare in the Appendix at the end of this book.

Paper

There are two basic choices of paper for a print on demand printing service.

'White' is similar to office photocopier paper with a smooth finish and bright white colour. The paper in this book is 'white'.

'Creme' is similar to the paper used in most paperback novels. It has a rough finish and is an off white colour.

Some companies do offer different paper weights, measured in gsm or grams per square metre. Office paper is usually 70 or 80 gsm, business cards are about 260 to 300 gsm. In a book, 100 gsm feels quite thick. Remember that choosing 100 gsm paper over 70 gsm will add about 50% to the thickness and weight of your book.

As with the other elements of book production, look on your own book shelf and choose a format that you like.

If you are unsure, you can have proof copies produced using different paper types so that you can make a direct comparison. Most printers will be able to send you samples too, both of paper and of finished books.

Cover Design

Any authors worry about cover design more than the content of the book. Certainly it is important to have a cover that sells the book by making it look appealing and interesting, and unfortunately, many browsers do judge a book by its cover.

If your book will compete with other similar books in this way, cover design is vital. However, there is no single 'best' cover design. If someone is looking for a book to read on holiday, they might narrow their preference down to romance, crime, horror or historical fiction and then browse within that section. They might look for something new from their favourite authors, in which case it doesn't matter how good your cover looks.

If you are selling your book on the merit of its content, and readers are specifically shopping for your book, then it doesn't matter how good other books' covers are, they are not the books that your readers are looking for.

The more effective your marketing, the less important cover design is, from a sales point of view.

Cover design is always important from a design and personality point of view. How the cover looks and feels tells the reader what to expect from your book. Should they expect simplicity, sophistication, elegance, surprise, intrigue, quality or something else?

The cover and the title together create an invitation for a reader to open your book. The content inside must then fulfil the expectations that you have raised in the reader's mind.

The actual cover design is a little more complex than it might appear, so if you are going to design a cover yourself, it is definitely worth getting help from a designer or publisher.

Firstly, the file that goes off to the printer looks different to the printed cover. It is bigger than the cover, and it has special printing marks that allow the printer to precisely align the cover with the 'text block', the inner pages of the book.

Because the cover wraps around the spine of the book, the spine width has to be calculated accurately so that the spine text as well as the front and back text are centred.

Finally, the cover needs a barcode so that wholesalers and retailers can process the book.

There are no rules about cover design. You could draw a picture, take a photograph, even have a plain white cover with just a title and barcode, it really is entirely up to you.

Here are some examples of books that we have published. The colour covers don't show up so well in black and white, so the ISBN numbers are included for you to look up the books at your favourite online book retailer.

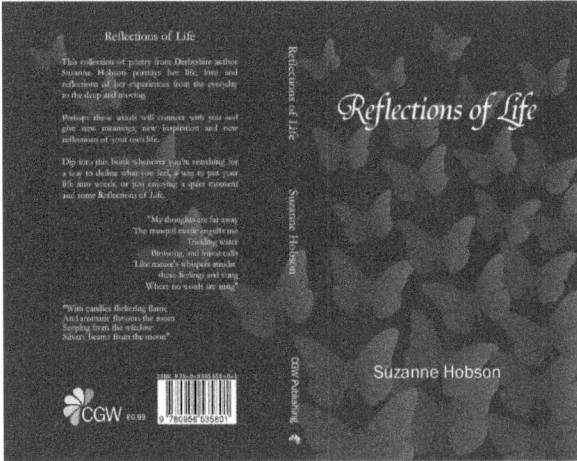

978-0-9565358-0-1

978-0-9565358-1-8

978-0-9565358-2-5

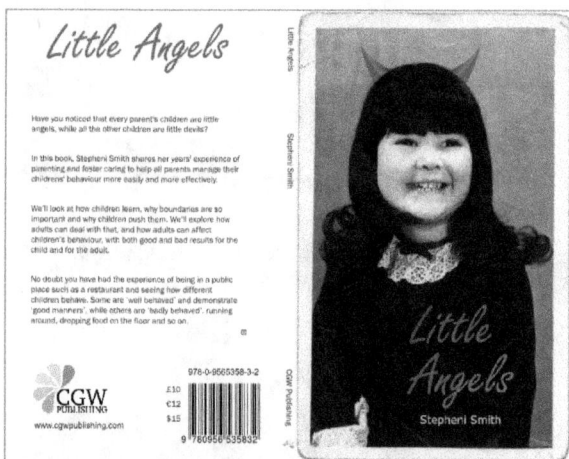

978-0-9565358-6-3

Contracts

A contract is a legally binding agreement between two or more parties which sets out rights and obligations, scope and term. In other words, what one person supplies to the other, what they get in return, for how long and covering what activities or markets.

An author might sign a contract with one publisher for Europe and a different publisher for Australia, and each would confer publishing rights within that territory only.

An author might sign a contract with an agent so that the agent is the author's legal representative in all matters relating to current and future book sales, but the contract might exclude audio books and training programs.

The golden rule with any contract is only to sign what you understand.

You will find an example publishing contract in the Appendix at the end of this book.

Copyright, Profits and Royalties

Copyright is a legal principle that protects the value of your creativity.

If your business was, say, making jewellery, how would you feel if someone walked into your studio and took all of your stock? You invested your money in raw materials, you invested your time in making the jewellery and you invested your creativity in the designs. How would you feel about someone taking that and giving you nothing in return?

On the other hand, how would you feel about someone coming in to your studio and buying some pieces that you had made?

And finally, how would you feel about someone coming in and saying, "These are wonderful, I'd like to sell them in my shop. I propose to pay you 50% of what you have priced them at, and in return I'll buy 20 pieces a month from you"?

In this example, you're trading a reduced price for guaranteed sales. You're not giving something away for nothing.

When you have a physical, tangible product, it's easy to see how you would protect its value and ensure you're properly compensated when someone else wants to enjoy it. When a customer wants to enjoy your jewellery for five minutes, looking in your shop window, there's no charge. When they want to enjoy it for life, they pay you a fair price for that enjoyment.

If they took your work and copied it for their friends, their friends would be able to enjoy it and you would get nothing in return.

When you're copying music and films, it's easy to see the big studios as 'greedy', but when you are the copyright holder for your own work, you can see more clearly the value of your creativity and why that is worth protecting.

This principle is absolutely central to the idea of copyright and royalty payments. Someone is paying you for the right to enjoy your creative work, as and when they want to.

Copyright is automatic in all written work. However, that doesn't make it easy to prove if you ever have to.

You cannot copyright an idea, as this would give you a monopoly, so copyright only covers the expression of an idea. If we take the idea of 'Boy meets girl, they fall in love, it ends in tears' then 'Romeo and Juliet' and 'Love Story' are each different expressions of this idea and each has a copyright that belongs to its author.

As an author, the most important thing you have is copyright, so you must make sure you understand the implications of signing away your right to copyright.

No publisher should ever ask for copyright ownership of your work, the publisher merely licences the right to produce copies of your work. In other words, the author is the only person who is legally permitted to make copies of his or her original work.

The author may allow other people to make copies under certain circumstances, for example:

- A publisher wishes to sell the book

- A training company wishes to use some of the author's material in their training notes

- A company wishes to use some of the author's poems on a calendar

- A charity wishes to use the author's work to inspire their volunteers

- A school wishes to use the author's work in one of their lessons

Some authors feel flattered when someone wants to use their copyrighted material, and they give it away for free, just because someone likes it and wants to use it. If someone wants to use your copyrighted material, it's because they value it and if they value it, they need to give you something of value in return. That doesn't always mean that they have to pay for it, there may be other things that you are prepared to trade.

The most important thing is to ensure that your copyright is protected, so as a minimum, you would expect anyone using your material to always show your copyright statement along with your original work.

It is entirely up to the author to decide what the terms of a copyright licence will be, but it is always a good idea to have some kind of licence contract in place. As a minimum, the author should send an email or letter with a statement like this:

"I hereby grant St Fred's School a non-exclusive licence to make copies of pages 1 through 12 of my book, "How to start your own business" for the sole purpose of using my material in your school lessons. You are not permitted to distribute copies of this material outside of St Fred's School. This copyright licence is granted on 1st January 2010 and expires on 31st December 2020. No payment is required for this licence on the condition that my original copyright notice appears on all copies made. By making copies of my material you implicitly agree to these terms."

If you do want to charge for the licence, you need to specify what licence fee is payable. For example, you might charge a one-off payment, or you might charge per copy made.

What you're basically saying is that the person you're granting a licence to keeps the copies to themselves and protects your copyright.

No-one in their right mind would have a problem with this, because they would recognise the hard work and creativity that has gone into your copyrighted material. After all, that's exactly why they want to copy it!

It's worth considering any request to use your material, because that increases your visibility, gives you something to tell other people about and also brings new marketing ideas that you can use yourself.

Royalties

When an author licences his or her copyright to a publisher, the publisher pays the author for the use of that licence. This payment is known as a royalty.

You may have heard of authors receiving an 'advance'. This is simply an advance payment of royalties, so the author receives their royalty percentage as a single, up front payment. The publisher is making the payment against anticipated book sales, and so the publisher often reduces this risk by capping the author's royalty payment. If the book sells more copies than the original advance was based on, the author often receives no further payments.

A publisher only buys the rights to publish a book, so copyright still rests with the author. The copyright makes it illegal for anyone to produce copies of the book. Essentially, copyright is the right to copy. This is not restricted to producing copies for sale, so someone who photocopies a page of your book for sharing with their family is breaking copyright law as much as someone who is selling illegally produced copies of your book.

When an author licences the publishing rights to a publisher, they form a contract which covers where the book may be sold and what the payment to the author will be. Traditional publishers expect to pay the author about 3% of the cover price of the book in royalties.

The traditional publisher has such a high cost of production and sale that there isn't much left over for the author, however they expect high sales volumes to make up for that.

The publisher pays for marketing out of the profits from book sales. In reality, they are using your book to market their publishing business. By launching new books regularly, they have a reason to announce something new to the press.

Most businesses have to advertise because they aren't doing something newsworthy. Publishers can get their new releases into the literature section of a newspaper, they can send books for review to magazines, they can send press releases, they can put the author on the radio and TV. The author's work is a marketing event for the publisher and it means that they don't have to advertise their general services in the way that most businesses have to.

If the author publishes the book themselves, they might expect to see the printing cost being only 20% of the cover price of the book, so it appears that they are making 80% profit. However, this doesn't account for the cost of distributing the book or the marketing costs that are necessary to get readers to buy the book.

When you add the costs of postage and packaging, marketing and the author's time, the profit on a book might be only 50%, which means that the author has to sell 17 times as many books through a traditional publisher to make the same profit.

The author will generally give copies away and sell copies at discounted prices, so the actual profits are even lower. A publisher gives the author more opportunity to market the book, reach a larger audience and sell more copies.

Everyone who is involved in the publishing of a book gets paid for a different part of that process.

The author gets paid for their creativity and for their time and skill in expressing that creativity.

The retailer gets paid for bringing customers into their shop to buy whatever products they can make a profit from.

The wholesaler makes a profit by buying in bulk from a manufacturer and holding stock on behalf of retailers.

The printer turns the raw materials of paper and ink into a finished book.

The publisher takes the author's raw work, turns it into a form suitable for printing and helps to market the book so that it becomes successful.

Let's look at a typical example.

A book that retails for £10 might cost around £2 to print.

A wholesale discount can be anything from 0% to 60%, but for small volumes, 20% is typical.

The retailer buys from the wholesaler, so we don't need to worry about their discount once the book has been sold to the wholesaler. Some retailers buy direct from the publisher, and their discount is the same as for the wholesaler.

This leaves £5.50 to be split between the publisher and author. A traditional publishing house would pay the author about 3% of the cover price or 30p, leaving £5.20 for marketing and the publisher's profits.

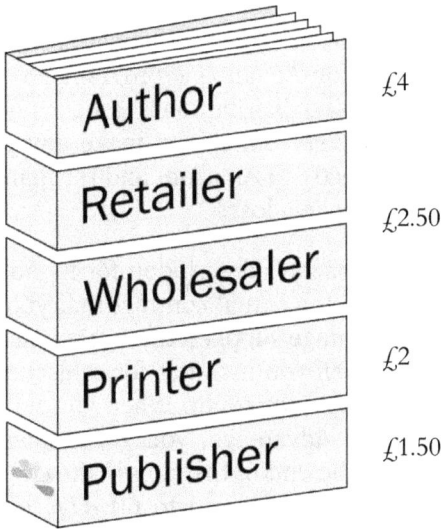

Author	£4
Retailer	£2.50
Wholesaler	
Printer	£2
Publisher	£1.50

Total retail price: £10

At CGW Publishing, we retain the minority share of the profit from the book for title management and marketing support, because we focus on authors who are using their books to build service businesses. We help the author to build a business using their book, so advertising the book is not in itself the most important way to do that. Let's say that CGW Publishing retains 15% or £1.50.

In this example, that leaves £4 for the author.

Of course, the reader doesn't always pay the full price for the book. Some book shops, especially online retailers, offer books at a discounted price. As with all 'cut price' retailers, they expect to retain their sales margins whilst passing the discount onto the manufacturer.

For example, Amazon expects to buy at 60% off cover price in its 'Amazon Advantage' program. Even if the author handles distribution and publishing themselves, it is very difficult to make any profit at all by selling directly to Amazon, and for many titles, the author will make a loss.

If you look at Amazon's description for its Advantage program, or even the actual contract that you sign to become an Advantage supplier, there is no mention of the discount. When you list titles for sale, there is no mention of Amazon's discount. When you sell a book through Amazon Advantage, you get a sales report and payment at the end of the month after the month of the sale, which can be up to 60 days later, and that's when you find out that their discount was 60%.

The exposure of selling through Amazon is generally not worth the cost to the author when you can also sell through Amazon at 0% discount. The only difference is that, at 0% discount, Amazon will show a book as '1 to 2 weeks delivery' whereas at 60% discount the book will show '24 hour delivery'.

If someone wants to buy your book, this may discourage them from buying it from Amazon, but they generally won't buy someone else's book instead because your book is a unique product, not a commodity.

Selling Your Book

The retailer is the person or company who directly sells your book to the customer; the person who actually buys the book to read themselves or perhaps as a gift.

Some authors think that by selling their book themselves from their own website, they keep the discounts that they would otherwise have to give to retailers.

Unfortunately, without the help of retailers, authors would simply never reach a big enough market to sell their book, even with the best website and Internet marketing expertise.

The mainstream, generic book retailers are so closely aligned with the mainstream, traditional publishers that many authors will not find them to be their most valuable retail channel.

Specialist book shops and retailers that have a specific interest in the subject of a book are a much better option for most authors, because the retailer's customers are already likely to be interested in your book. All you have to do is let them know about it.

High Street Book Shops

Many authors dream of walking into their local book shop and seeing their own book for sale there.

The reality is that your book will be there for one of two reasons.

Firstly, if a major publishing house has picked up your book and is currently promoting it.

Secondly, if you have convinced the manager of the shop to hold a stock of your books.

The major book retail chains own very little of their actual shelf space – it is owned by the major publishing houses, and those publishers place the books that they want the public to buy.

Given the number of books actually in print, the chances of someone buying a particular book when they are 'just browsing' are tiny.

At airport book shops the problem is even more obvious – people browse for something that they will read on holiday and probably leave in the hotel room, and they will make a decision based almost entirely on product placement. The whole idea of a best seller list convinces people that a book must be worth reading and, for the majority of books, the content has been forgotten as soon as the reader's sun tan has worn off.

Independent book shops are much more likely to hold a stock of a book if it has local interest or if the author is prepared to do some local marketing to drive customers into the shop. While the independent book shop has more control over what they stock, the principles are the same in that they will stock what they believe they can sell.

Some book shops specialise in particular markets, for example in religious, technical or local history books. If you write in a particular niche area, it's always useful to seek out specialist book shops and ask them to hold stock.

Therefore, while a book in the High Street is a dream of most authors, it is not the most important way to market a book because, by the time someone goes into the shop to ask for your book, your marketing has already succeeded.

Online Retailers

The major High Street book shops also have online shops, because they need to compete with the retailers who operate only online. Amazon is probably the best known of the online retailers.

Amazon is a book shop like any other. There are more books in the world than would fit into any bookshop. Some are in stock for you to take away, others you have to order.

The main difference between an online book shop and a 'real' book shop is the physical building. Online book shops therefore sell fewer books to 'browsers', so they use their own best seller lists and recommendations to sell books to site visitors.

A customer is more likely to go into a real book shop and browse for a book to buy as a gift or to read on holiday.

A customer is more likely to go to an online book shop to buy a specific book, expecting to pay less for it.

Therefore, you need to market your book differently through these two types of retailer.

With an online retailer, you need to develop your own methods of getting customers to buy the book online. For example, you would develop your own website and direct visitors who want to buy the book to a number of online retailers so they could choose where to buy the book. Most people who buy online already have accounts set up with a particular retailer, so it's good to give them that choice.

With a 'real' book shop, you are aiming your book at browsers, so product placement is vital.

To see how the retail process works, let's compare an independent retailer, Brian's Books with an online retailer such as Amazon.

A customer walks into Brian's Books and picks up a book off the shelf, takes it to the till, pays for it and walks out with it.

A customer walks into Brian's Books and he doesn't have the book in stock. The customer asks him to order it, he orders it from the wholesaler or publisher and they send it to him. He calls the customer to say it's arrived, the customer goes to the shop, pays for the book and walks out with it.

A customer visits Amazon's online shop, orders and pays for the book. Amazon send it either from their own stock or order it from the wholesaler. A few days later, the book arrives in the post. The customer has no idea whether Amazon had the book in their warehouse or whether they had to order it in.

If Amazon don't expect to sell many copies of a book, based on their own sales figures, they will order books one at a time from the wholesaler. As soon as you start selling tens of books through Amazon, they'll want a small stock which means they can supply orders quicker, which makes a customer more likely to buy from them than from a local book shop.

Everyone in the chain sells the book for more than they buy it for. By cutting out Amazon and selling books yourself, you have their profit as well as your own, but you have to supply the postage and packaging, and you have to use up your time handling orders, taking payment, addressing envelopes and going to the post office.

Since the profits you make on book sales are a source of income, you should be declaring all of this on your tax return too.

The discounts offered to the wholesalers and retailers are there to help them make a profit so that they continue to market books, which keeps the book market moving for all authors to benefit from.

Specialist Retailers

If you've written a book on electric guitars, approach guitar shops. They will be open to other products that they can sell at a profit, because not everyone who comes into their shop will actually walk out with a guitar.

If you've written a book on team building, approach companies that sell products for trainers and consultants, and approach the HR departments of companies that will run their own team events.

If you're written a poetry book, approach gift shops, because poetry books are very often bought to be given as presents.

Any retailer is always looking for new products to sell, because they want to offer more to their regular customers. They want to keep their stock fresh so that the people who walk by their windows see something new to buy. If their customers keep seeing the same stock, they'll stop going into the shop.

If you can help draw customers into the shop too, so much the better. Organise a signing event and talk and publicise it in the local press. Anything that brings customers to the retailer makes the retailer more likely to stock your book.

If your book is relevant, most retailers will be happy to take a small stock on a 'sale or return' basis, meaning that they only pay for the books when they sell them, and if they don't sell them, they give them back to you.

This seems like a very good idea, and a good way to persuade the retailer to take some books, until you realise that you can't do anything with the dirty, dog eared copies that you get back at the end of the sale or return period. Therefore, don't be afraid to push back on the retailer. You could say that only half the copies ordered can be returned, or you can set a time limit, or you can specify that any copies returned must be in a saleable condition.

Give the retailer a written receipt with these conditions on, and when the time limit is up, you can either get your books back, or you can make sure the retailer pays you for them in the event that they sold them and forgot to let you know.

Marketing Events

The launch of a new book is an event that the media and book shops are interested in, because it is news worthy.

To sell your book successfully through High Street shops, product placement is vital. This simply means that the shop needs to put your book where potential buyers will see it.

Good locations include:

- In the window

- On a table just inside the door

- On the book shelves but facing towards the customer rather than end on

To get a book shop owner or manager to take a stock of your books and put them in a good location within the shop, you need to give them something that brings them customers.

If the shop has a website, link to it from yours and make them your preferred supplier for online orders.

Offer the shop a signing event where you spend a morning or evening at the book shop, talking to customers and selling signed copies. You might also give a talk or lecture, depending on the content of your book.

The event can be publicised in the local press and on local radio and TV stations, which creates publicity that brings people into the shop to buy your book. This has a huge impact on the shop's marketing exposure, so you can expect good placement in return for your efforts.

You may be thinking that the local media aren't interested in your book, but they definitely are.

The local media make money from advertising, but to do that, they have to give their audience valuable news and information.

A newspaper has a regular print run which creates pressure on editors and journalists to fill space with news. They will sell some space to advertisers, but the majority has to carry information that the reader will value.

Radio and TV stations are under the same pressure to fill time on daytime talk shows.

Therefore, editors are waiting to hear from you, because you give them exactly what they are looking for. Instead of having to go out and find news, you are bringing it to them.

Marketing Your Business

If you have a product business, you produce something tangible to sell to your customers. You make a profit by adding value to raw materials, for example by turning them into jewellery, and the profit pays for the time that it takes you to produce the products.

When you make the products yourself, your income is limited by the time you have available for manufacturing. Selling products takes time too, so your need for a particular level of income dictates your product price.

If it takes you a day to make a particular piece of jewellery, you have to charge a day's worth of time for it, regardless of the profit on it, and it has to be good enough for someone to pay that price. If you need £50 a day to live and the cost of raw materials is £1 then you have to charge £51 for the piece.

If it takes you five minutes, you can produce a large stock in a day and the unit price can be lower. Let's say that you make 50 in a day and that the raw materials cost £1 per piece. Now you can afford to charge £2 per piece, assuming that you sell them all.

After you have established sales channels, you create a system where pieces that you have already made are being sold at the same time as you are making new pieces. The income from sales pays for your costs of time and raw materials.

If you have a service business, there is no physical product to sell your customers. Service businesses supply services such as:

- Management consulting

- Training

- Domestic cleaning

- Decorating

- Accountancy

- Car valeting

With a service business, you have spent time learning skills or knowledge which now have value for your clients. The end result of your service is some improvement in your client's business or life, for example increased business efficiency or a clean house. This end result is a quality of something that the client already owns, rather than something completely new.

Generally, your service is not something that your client cannot do for themselves, it is something that they have a good reason for not doing themselves. Their reasons may include:

- They don't have time, or their time is more profitably spent elsewhere

- They want the security of having something done 'properly' e.g. tax returns

They don't feel that their skills are at the level of someone who provides the service on a daily basis

They want to bring new perspectives and ideas into their business

They think that their staff will value external opinions over those of their managers

They want to learn from someone who they recognise as a specialist in a particular field

Therefore, when you are selling services, it's useful to remember that you are not selling something that is totally unique and beyond your client's reach, you are selling your ability to add value to your client's business or life.

There are three very important differences between a product business and a service business.

1. With a service business, the customer can't try the product out before they buy it.

2. With a service business, your profit is limited by your time.

3. With a service business, the supplier can't take the service back if the client doesn't pay for it.

When the customer can try the product before buying it, they have confidence in the product itself.

With a service, the client has to make a judgement based on other criteria.

If the service doesn't meet the client's needs, the service provider has still spent their time providing that service, so the costs are the same even when the client isn't happy. When a customer isn't happy with a product, they can return it and you can sell it to someone else.

Some clients take advantage of this situation and dispute the quality of a service provided, knowing that the service provider can't untrain their staff, put the dirt back in their house or take back their company accounts.

If you provide any kind of service, it is therefore important that you check what you are delivering to the client at every stage of the sales process and work out a payment schedule that protects your investment in time whilst giving the client confidence in their decision.

Contracts are important, but they do not win you new clients.

Passive Income

The notion of 'passive income' is something that Internet marketers have been talking about for years. They promise to show you the secrets of making money while you sleep. You'll wake up, check your bank balance and find that people have been to your website and given you money while you have been counting sheep.

What the marketers are doing is appealing to the biggest problem for any self employed service business; that your income is limited by your time. You can't spend every working hour delivering your service, because you need to spend at least some of your time on administration, marketing, sales and other activities that are necessary in running a business. Unfortunately, delivering your service is the only thing that you get paid for.

The only real way to significantly grow a service business is to hire employees. Other than that, you could charge more for your services or outsource administration. These still don't solve the problem that your time is limited, and therefore your income is limited.

Creating information products that you can mass produce is one way to generate income that is not dependent on your time, and 'passive income' is the ultimate aim.

Unfortunately, income is anything but passive.

In order to sell books you have to invest time and money. You have to write the book, publish it, market it, set up sales channels and you have to push those sales channels to sell your book. If you are looking for a 'get rich quick' scheme, then the only people getting rich are the Internet marketers who have signed you up to their passive income mentoring program.

Let's say that your business is corporate training. Almost without exception, you have to sell each and every training program that you deliver. It's time consuming, so you have to charge a high enough price for design and delivery to cover the cost of all the sales you don't win.

If you write a book about a subject that you train, you can use it as a marketing tool. It gives you credibility, and that makes it easier to sell your training programs. In return, that makes it easier to sell more copies of your book. The two complement each other.

It sounds tempting, but there is no such thing as 'passive' income.

Credibility

Credibility is the single most important thing that a service business needs in order to succeed.

Service businesses try to demonstrate credibility with case studies, testimonials, high quality brochures, staff uniforms and other tangible signs of an established business.

A book not only impresses potential clients, it is also a unique way to package the intellectual property that is the foundation of your business.

Some authors worry that, if they give away their ideas in a book, the client will just buy the book and not their services.

This is exactly why you would use the book as a sales and marketing tool, as part of a methodical approach to winning new clients, and not just give the book away to anyone who asks for it.

Some people won't buy your services because they think they can do better themselves. They are perfect readers for your book.

Some people will buy your book as a result of using your services, because they want to find out more about the subject.

Some people will want to buy your services, but will need to be convinced of your credibility, and they are the people who will read your book as part of a sales process.

A book gives the author credibility, so a business book is a very valuable asset to use in building a service business. Anyone can write a glossy brochure but a book is a unique way to convey your ideas which will make a far better impression than almost anything else you can do.

When a brochure costs only 50p to print, it's easy to send them out to anyone who asks for one and also to many people who didn't ask. It's easy to go to conferences and give them out to anyone who passes by. It's easy, when someone says, "Send us a brochure and we'll keep it on file", to think that they'll do anything with it other than file it in the bin.

If a brochure or business card cost £2 to print, would you give them out as readily?

A book might cost £2 to print, so think of it as a very valuable brochure. It makes you think harder about who you might give it to, and it makes you follow up with them to make sure they are reading it. As a minimum, you expect their feedback on the book itself. You have given them something of value and you can expect value in return.

One of the benefits of having a book is that it gives you an event to market. Marketing your business is a difficult activity because the mainstream media sell advertising space and so don't give it away for free when you're not doing anything news worthy.

Launching a book and being able to offer the media something for their audience, such as a regular column or books to give as competition prizes is newsworthy. A book gives you something to announce, and news will always be more valuable to the reader than advertising.

Your book contains your personality, so if you send it to someone who is considering using your services, if they like your book then they'll probably like you. If they don't then you have saved time; your most valuable asset.

Therefore, a book will lend credibility to your business, help you to qualify potential customers and lead to better relationships between you and your clients. By using your book properly, you will grow your service business, and by growing your service business, you will develop the brand and reputation which will help you to sell more books.

What's Wrong With Ebooks?

There are two types of ebook; electronic versions of published books and Internet marketing adverts that aim to mimic the credibility of a properly published book.

A published book which is subsequently made available electronically for readers to read on a computer or specialised ebook reading device is a useful way of increasing book sales alongside audio books and different printed formats.

Once you have published your book, you should consider producing an ebook version to exploit alternative sales channels and reader preferences.

Ebook formats include:

- Amazon Kindle

- Apple iBooks (epub format)

- PDF (Portable Document Format)

- Microsoft Reader

Using ebooks as a marketing tool is a current trend in Internet marketing which serve as a low cost way to emulate the credibility of a published book.

Ebooks appear to cost nothing to give out, so they are generally worth nothing. They don't add credibility and they don't significantly add value to your business.

Only use an ebook to impart genuine information to your clients so that you improve your service overall.

For example, if you feel you spend a lot of time answering the same questions, write a short 'Q&A' document and put it on your website or send it out by email. Whatever you do, don't tell your customers that it has any intrinsic value.

The Internet has become a trading platform for anyone who wants to set up their own business, and Internet marketing makes it difficult to distinguish a legitimate business from one that has set up overnight with no track record.

This may sound harsh, but as a rule of thumb, if someone is offering an ebook and trying to convince you that it has an intrinsic value, it's because their ideas are simply not worth the cost of publishing. If their ideas really were worth $100, they would be selling them for real money.

Companies have always produced buyer's guides, catalogues, white papers and brochures which are designed to get potential customers to buy.

Over the past few years, the ebook has proliferated as a vehicle for educating potential buyers, and therefore influencing their buying decision.

Ebooks usually go hand in hand with other Internet marketing approaches such as 'articles' written solely for the purpose of exploiting search engines and driving visitors to sites based not on their merit and relevancy but on their marketing budget.

Search for anything on the Internet that it's possible to buy and you'll come across dozens of examples of websites that use articles and ebooks in this way.

While you may think that these methods are acceptable, our view is that they should not be part of any serious, credible business strategy, because:

- These methods are used specifically to exploit the way that Internet search engines work, therefore they are designed to 'get round the rules' rather than to provide genuinely valuable information.

- These methods drive visitors to a website artificially, so their disappointment will be greater if they don't find what they're looking for. Consequently, they also give genuine customers the wrong impression about the website.

Would you buy a Rolex watch if their marketing slogan was "Buy one get one free"? Would you buy from Rolls Royce if their message was "Sale must end Friday!!!"?

A common format for an ebook is "The ten biggest mistakes people make in..." which roughly translates as "The ten biggest mistakes you'll make by not buying from us".

An alternative is the "How to choose a..." format. It's the same message, packaged as information rather than a warning. Would you buy a house based on a "How to choose your new home" ebook produced by an estate agent? Probably not. But if you were putting your house on the market, and an estate agent gave you a "Tips for selling your house" booklet, would you sign up with them? Perhaps not as a direct result, but you might be influenced by it.

If their booklet was obviously promoting their own services and attacking their competitors, would you still feel positive about their services?

Buyers guides are valuable, but they have to be impartial. Articles are valuable, and they do bring more visitors to your website, but they have to be unbiased and informative, not just thinly disguised adverts.

The golden rule of Internet marketing is "Content is King". That's genuine content, not sales pitch masquerading as content.

As the search engines get better at filtering out 'fake' content, Internet marketers will respond with new methods, so you can expect this situation to be continually evolving.

Internet marketing is of course vital to raise your website's visibility. However, there are legitimate and ethical ways of achieving this, and there are unethical ways. The Search Engines constantly refine their indexing methods to counteract the unethical marketing methods, favouring the legitimate, relevant, valuable websites.

Focus on providing valuable information for your readers and you will always succeed.

Social Media Marketing

Web 2.0 is a phrase coined by Internet experts for a new generation of applications that centre around increased interactivity.

This move from static to interactive websites led to a completely new way of interacting with other Internet users, including Blogs, Wikis, Discussion Forums, Social Networking, Social Bookmarking, Online Communities and Lifestreaming.

What these mean for users is that site owners no longer drive content. Site owners provide a structure or forum and visitors provide content through their own discussions, experiences and interests.

Some of the most popular and well known social media websites include:

Wikipedia - A user maintained and peer reviewed online encyclopedia

Facebook - A community that connects 'friends' and lets them send messages and play games together

Second Life - A virtual world where users can interact with each other in various ways

MySpace - An online community similar to Facebook

Delicious - A service that allows users to mark websites that they want to share with other users

Blogger - A web logging or 'blogging' site that allows users to maintain their own news pages

Twitter - A 'micro blogging' site that allows users to send short messages within peer communities

As new Internet tools gain popularity, many marketing experts advise the use of social websites to create publicity and therefore sales.

The news – in newspapers, on TV and on Internet news feeds – is written by professional journalists and critically assessed by editors before it reaches the reader or viewer.

Over the last few years, social media platforms have made the news accessible to everyone. When the public demand more immediate news, the news agencies use video footage, photographs and commentary from the public.

News agencies have always used eye witness reports for 'fast breaking' stories. The images may be compelling, but the frantic, disjointed commentary of an eye witness at the scene of a disaster does not have the same value as that of an objective, professional journalist.

Quality is sacrificed for immediacy.

The Evolution of the Internet

In the old days of the Internet, if you wanted to sell something, you created a website that was essentially an online brochure and you waited for people to come and read it.

The rise of email marketing meant that, when you had someone's email address, you could let them know your latest news. Businesses used it to communicate special offers and events.

But then spam came along, and email inboxes all over the world filled up with adverts for products that nobody wanted, and scams, and con tricks, and viruses and all manner of unwelcome things.

Why? Because that's the nature of any uncontrolled, unregulated marketplace.

Spam filters evolved to block spam, and spammers evolved ways to get your email address even when you hadn't given it to them, which they sold to other spammers. Companies that legitimately need your email address had to fight through growing anti spam measures; everything from email filters to Data Protection laws.

As the usage of email increased, people's inboxes began to overflow, not with spam but now with news from their growing circle of friends. In the old days, when people left school or university, they kept in touch with a small number of friends.

Now, when people leave school, they can keep in touch forever with email addresses, no matter where in the world they go. And that means that they get the latest news from people who, in the past, they wouldn't care to hear from.

With email, you might just ignore or even block messages from people you don't want to hear from. But that takes time, so what people started to do was ignore everything, just like they throw away all of the 'junk mail' that comes through their front door.

Web Logs, or 'Blogs', appeared as personal news sites. You could write a Blog and it would be like having your own personal newspaper, and your visitors would come and find out what you had to say.

However, Blogs then proliferated to the point that there are too many to read.

The problem with news is that when there's too much of it, nothing is newsworthy. When everything is news, nothing is news.

But on the other hand, younger generations do like to keep in touch with a growing circle of friends. They like to know where their friends are and what they're up to. They like to know that Jimmy has just had a cheese sandwich and Susie has just got on the bus. It's like being with your friends, chattering, but not actually being with them. It's social noise. It lets us know we're in a community, even though we're physically surrounded by strangers. So rather than talk to strangers, it's easier to relate to the stream of noise coming from your friends.

People become more isolated, more a citizen of 'Cyberspace' than of the real world.

Imagine if every person you had ever met and every shop you had ever bought from was shouting their news at you. How would anything stand out from the background noise?

Blogs take time to write and time to read, and when there are too many to read there's not enough time. Why write a 200 word Blog when you could get your thoughts across in 140 letters? Micro blogging is an evolution of regular blogging, so instead of writing an essay, just write "I've just seen the news about XYZ Co", or, "I'm having a cheese sandwich. It's nice".

Twitter is the most popular micro blogging site. Celebrities share the fact that they're just getting in or out of taxis, and the general public share their reactions to those gripping news items.

Facebook and Myspace are the two most popular social networking sites. They aim to replicate face to face social interaction, and originally they served to answer the question, "I wonder what Fred's doing now?" They allowed the general public to tell the world what they're up to, and for the general public to interact with them in return. You can read someone's news, see their photos, write messages to them and play games with them. It's just like being with all your friends while you're still sitting at your desk, getting paid for it.

The evolution of the Internet means that everyone is shouting at the same time. It's just the same as walking into a crowded market with all the traders selling the same products at the same prices and all trying to shout louder than the others.

Walk into a market in certain parts of the world and you'll immediately be inundated with offers from boys who will be your guide, take you to the reputable shops, protect you from the crooks and stop you from being ripped off.

In the same way, Internet marketing experts can help you to get your message heard above the noise. They can give you 'Search Engine Optimisation', which is basically a series of methods for tricking search engines into displaying a website more often than it deserves from its own merit.

They can write articles and ebooks, give you social media campaigns and use the latest methods to drive visitors to your website.

Of course, once you realise that the market guide took you to his uncle's shop and you paid ten times what something was actually worth, you might feel that you had been ripped off. The guide, literally, saw you coming.

Imagine how your visitors will feel when they realise they have been tricked into looking at your website.

It's much better to attract visitors, fair and square. The old methods still work; relevant, high quality information, honest sales messages and links with relevant and valuable websites.

Collapsing Markets

Imagine a country of deep valleys divided by dense forest. In each valley, a tribe lives happily, growing enough food for its population. As a population grows beyond the resources available to support it, hunters have to go outside of the valley. They go to other tribes and trade for their resources. One tribe grows wheat, the other rice. It's an equal exchange.

What happens when one tribe wants more but doesn't have anything to trade? Typically, they take what they want by force. Or, once the civilisation has created the concept of territory, they invade another tribe and make it part of their own, absorbing its resources. Unfortunately, another way to make scarce resources go further is to do away with the inhabitants of the competing tribe.

Import and export are vital to sustain any kind of economy, and when tribes have nothing to export, they can't import. By protecting territory, a tribe protects its claim to natural resources, be they gold, diamonds, rice, water or sunshine, and that gives the tribe something to export.

The bottom end of the business market is flooded with small tribes, each trying to gain a foot hold by feeding off each other.

If a business has real value, it will have more customers than suppliers. It will export more than it imports. It will earn more from its customers than it pays its suppliers, and that difference is its profit. Profit is the fundamental difference between a business and a hobby.

When a business buys more than it sells, consumes more than it supplies, it makes a loss and ultimately fails. When a country imports more than it exports, this is known as a 'trade deficit'. In order for any business or economy to survive, there must be profit.

When a business has little intrinsic value, it can get into an ever decreasing circle of cannibalisation.

For example, Twitter allows you to follow other people's news as well as providing news for other people to follow.

If you have real intrinsic value, if you are saying something that is genuinely interesting, you will have more followers than 'followed'.

A King has many followers or subjects, but who does a King follow?

A football fan follows his or her team, but how many followers does the fan have?

Let's calculate news value[1] by looking at the ratio between how many people want to read about your news and how many people you want to read about.

If you read a newspaper story and tell ten of your friends about it, adding your own opinion to what you tell them, you have added value to the news.

If you read an article and tell no-one, you have made a negative contribution to the amount of news in the world. You have consumed news but created none.

The most popular British writer on Twitter, Stephen Fry[2], is following 53,497 people and is followed by 1,616,454 people.

This means that Stephen Fry generates 30 times more interesting thoughts than he consumes. Now let's use Stephen Fry as a the measure of newsworthiness and give him a value of 1 Fry.

The British comedian Bobby Ball of the duo Cannon and Ball, popular in the 1980s, is worth 10 Frys.

Jerry Springer, the American TV host, is worth 50 Frys. He contributes 50 times the amount of news as does Stephen Fry.

---

1   See the appendix for a full list of our results

2   According to someone on TV

Britney Spears, the American singer turned dropout, has over 5 Million followers, yet she is worth only 0.42 Frys.

Oprah Winfrey, the American TV talk show host, is worth 6,625 Frys, or 6.6 KiloFrys.

Paul O'Grady, the British comedian turned TV presenter and author, changes the picture quite significantly. He has only 13,340 followers, but he isn't following anyone. Zero. His value is infinite. An infinite number of Frys. But for the purposes of calculating a number, we must assume that he is somewhat interested in at least someone, so our formula gives him a value of 441 KiloFrys or 0.44 MegaFrys.

The singer David Bowie, by our formula, has a value of 1.54 MegaFrys. He contributes 1.54 Million times the news value of Stephen Fry.

At the other end of the scale, an Internet marketing guru in America, who has lectured at Harvard Business School on the value of Twitter to businesses, scores just 0.03 Frys or 30 MilliFrys.

She is followed by 59,427 people but is following 59,080 people, a difference of just 447. While Internet marketing 'experts' focus on the 59427, what we need to look at is the 447, because this indicates the value that the person adds.

Whilst you may think that having 59,427 people following you is good for publicity, the fact that she needs to follow 59,080 people in order to attract her followers is very bad indeed.

When Internet search engines first arrived to help people sift through the mass of websites, marketers quickly realised that, if your website appeared near the top of the search results, you attracted more visitors. For the same reason, if you look in most categories in the Yellow Pages, you'll find businesses called A1 or AAA or ABC.

When the search engine designers realised that site owners were artificially exploiting the indexing rules to gain an advantage, they changed the rules, and this evolution is still going on today. An important measure of a website's importance is how many other sites link to it. The simple rule of thumb is that if other site owners think that your website is valuable then it must be.

When site owners realised this, they created 'link farms'; long lists of links to each others' websites. Having a dozen websites all linking to each other does not make them valuable. Most search engines now discount link farming. A site becomes less valuable if it uses such methods to try to gain an unfair advantage.

The way that Twitter gurus advocate building a following is to say to each other, "Hey, if I follow you, will you follow me? It will be good for both of us!"

No, it won't.

If our tribe becomes cannibalistic because there is no trade with other tribes, it's no use saying, "Hey, if I eat your leg, you can eat mine!"

A closed, cannibalistic market is not a market at all because no-one can profit by more than what the other members are able to pay.

When websites link to each other in a 'link farm', they create a closed market which benefits no-one, although it might trick a unwary few visitors.

In the business world, such a closed market is called a cartel, and cartels are generally illegal because they take away consumer choice, and choice is one of the foundations of a market economy.

So far, we have looked at people who contribute news. The people who were interesting before Twitter appeared are still interesting. The people who try to manipulate Twitter to their own advantage are easy to spot, if you know what to look for.

The greater the difference between followers and following, the more interesting and newsworthy a person is.

These people contribute to the amount of valuable information in the world by amplifying the flow of news. News, by definition, is interesting, otherwise it doesn't get passed on.

What happens when people contribute anti-news by consuming more than they produce?

A British sales manager turned small business consultant and social media expert has 1,216 followers who enjoy reading about the fact that it's sunny today. He is following 1,235 people, so he produces less news than he consumes. His news value is less than zero Frys at -0.02 Frys, or -20

MilliFrys. What's worrying is that he advises businesses on the importance of social media marketing.

The smaller the number of Frys, the less interesting the person is. A negative number means that on top of being grossly uninteresting, the person actually detracts from the amount of news in the world.

An American Internet marketing guru who says that he "helps businesses to elevate their status in the online world to maximise their marketing exposure" as he "travels the world imparting his wisdom" is worth -0.05 Frys, or -50 MilliFrys.

His unnewsworthiness is surpassed only by the British singer and TV presenter, Cilla Black. She measures in at -1.76 Frys.

In fact, none of the Internet marketing gurus who we found advocating Twitter as the latest business marketing tool scored any higher than 9 MilliFrys, which is disappointing when you notice that Dick Van Dyke of "Cor blimey Mary Poppins!" fame scores just over 3 Frys.

A dancing chimney sweep is a factor of a thousand more important than the most successful Internet marketer.

This is especially disappointing if you have paid these people a lot of money to build a social media marketing campaign for you. You would literally be better off spending your money with a man who dances with penguins.

Internet marketers claim to show you the secrets to driving visitors to your website. What they offer is similar to the service offered by the young boys in the markets. If you hire your own market stall and they think you look a bit green, they will offer to bring the best customers to your stall. For a price.

What would you rather have? Customers who have been conned by a 'guide', or customers who find your stall as a result of their own decision and who genuinely value your products?

As you can see, creating valuable news is not an easy job. If you don't legitimately stand out from the background noise, you're not going to get there with marketing tricks either.

Many businesses, especially small businesses and sole traders, are jumping on social media such as Facebook and Twitter as marketing tools.

A simple calculation of the difference between creation and consumption, between import and export, immediately reveals who is actually creating value. And in any business, creating value is the way to make a living.

The key is to use these tools to create a genuine following. Don't simply follow other people, concentrate on saying something of real value.

Instead of shouting louder, focus on the people who are already listening with 'good old fashioned' marketing values:

- Focus on one thing that you do well

- Find your niche

- Create real value for your clients

- Keep working at it

When you consume more than you create, your business will not survive. In a market of cannibals, the best you can do is break even.

When you look around at your business associates and clients, and you're honest with yourself, who is gaining more? Are they feeding more from you than you are from them?

The danger is to seek a sense of belonging with like minded people, but they are ahead of you in the food chain. They'll see you like the boys in the market do, and they'll be only too happy to tell you exactly what you want to hear.

While not everyone is out to take advantage of you, just remember that there are no 'get rich quick' schemes. Real value is measured by the audience, not the broadcaster.

From Hobby to Business

The primary difference between a business and a hobby is money.

A hobby consumes money, a business generates it.

A hobby is something that you do for its own pleasure and in your own time, so the money that it costs is immaterial. You generally have a full time job that pays your cost of living, so the hobby doesn't need to generate income.

People in full time job often say, "I work for a living so that I can enjoy my hobbies".

Many people dream of making a living from their hobby, and it is certainly a reality in one form or another as long as you focus on it as a business.

Some people complain that turning their hobby into a business takes the enjoyment out of it, and this need not be the case.

However, in order to make a living, you must focus on income as the primary measure of success.

Many successful business owners enjoy what they do immensely. To achieve this, you need to value your own time above all else, so that you look at the best return on investment for your time.

For example, let's say that you have your own business and you have an hour to spare during the working day.

Do you spend it:

- Watching TV?

- Going to the shops?

- Tinkering with your website?

- Making follow up calls to clients?

- Looking for new clients?

Which is most valuable to you?

Watching TV costs nothing but creates no income. Going shopping costs money. Tinkering with your website saves you money that you might spend on website design. Making follow up calls keeps your existing clients happy, and they might spend more money with you. Looking for new clients brings you new sources of income.

When you are trying to make a living, you need to use every minute of your time as productively as possible. You might not like paying someone to maintain your website, but in the long run it costs you less than spending your valuable time doing it yourself.

A useful rule of thumb is to ask yourself, "Could anyone do this, or is it unique to me?"

Website? Any web designer could do it.

Sales? It's down to you.

Many people who turn a hobby into a business also have a problem with pricing. Because they know the 'true cost' of their product or service, they undervalue it and undercharge. Simply, they tend to set their prices based on production costs and ignore the value of their own time.

This is the case regardless of whether the business is jewellery or management consulting.

If it's jewellery, the business owner thinks, "But this cost me less than £1 to make, I can't sell it for £10!"

If it's management consulting, the business owner thinks, "But this is easy, I can't charge £1000 a day for it!".

There's a joke about management consultants, which is really an insult pretending to be a joke, which says that a management consultant is someone who borrows the client's watch to tell them the time.

If that's really the case, why isn't the client telling the time themselves? It's because they can't or they have a very good reason not to.

Just because you own a watch doesn't mean you can tell the time.

Many service businesses provide something that the customer could do for themselves, if they only had the time.

Therefore, business owners of both product and service businesses consistently undervalue their own time, and that is the reason why they fail.

The key to turning your hobby into a business is to remember and practice these simple rules:

- Focus on what has value to your customers

- Look at your competitors' prices and charge your market value

- Spend your time on the activities that need you

- Keep some spare time allocated to still enjoy what you do

- Above all else, know the value of your own time

The relevance of this to publishing? At CGW, we're not only publishing books, we're building businesses.

Your knowledge, experience and expertise has a value, and that's why it is called 'Intellectual Property'. You can't keep it under lock and key, and you can't sell it directly. However, you can use it to create products and services that you can sell directly, and you can then use those products and services to build your business.

This is part of our expertise at CGW. We help you to turn your intellectual property into something tangible and profitable, and we help you to build a reliable and sustainable business around it too.

Starting Your Business

If you do not already have a business then there are broadly three options for you. You can either continue as you are, you can become self employed or you can form a company.

If you are in the UK then you can register with HMRC as a sole trader, which is known as being 'self employed'.

The more complex way is to set up a company.

Running a business as a limited liability company used to have tax advantages, but not any longer.

It is possible to sell your copyright as an author to your company in order to realise some income from it, but in reality, unless your book sales are very high, HMRC or your country's tax office is unlikely to allow you a significant amount of money for this.

Whichever route you choose means that you will pay tax on your income from writing.

We can give you initial advice on how to go about this, and help you get started with your new business if you are not already trading.

CGW Publishing

CGW Publishing is an independent publisher, specialising in helping authors to develop a service business from their intellectual property.

Christopher Greenaway and Amelia Hartley built a successful management consultancy practice around their books and other information products, and now they work with authors who want to realise the potential of their own intellectual property.

CGW Publishing offers much more than a traditional publisher with a full writing, publishing and business development service for authors who want to get their ideas into print and then develop those ideas into a profitable business.

Some of the authors we work with write their own work and we edit and publish it, whilst we ghost write and publish for others.

We help authors convert their intellectual property and creativity into income, not only through short term book sales but by building a solid business foundation that helps the author to exploit their hard work and expertise as much as possible for as long as possible.

For example, one of our clients had delivered a lecture for a number of years on a particular subject and wanted to publish a book in the same field to build his reputation.

His idea for the book was fine, but the format and message was very different to that of the lecture. To continue with both as they were would mean that he would be dividing his attention between them and one would not directly complement the other.

We rewrote his lecture and adapted his book so that each conveyed the same message. The lecture sells the book, the book sells the lecture and together, they create the credibility that grows his brand and therefore his business.

We don't work with just anyone who wants to write a book. Our target clients are people who are building a service business on their own intellectual property and who we can work with to integrate writing and publishing into their marketing and business development activities.

A traditional publisher buys the rights to your book and pays you about 3% of profits for that. In return, they do whatever they want with the book in terms of appearance, marketing etc.

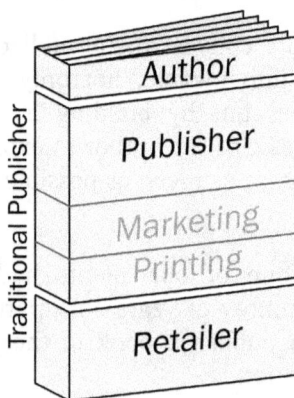

The publisher may pay you an advance against royalties, based on their expectations of book sales. They still expect you to sell the book, with signings, media interviews etc. Equally, they may never put your book into print at all.

With a traditional publisher, royalties are typically capped at the figure you receive as an advance, so if the book is more successful than the publisher anticipated, the author doesn't benefit.

A self publishing service such as Lulu or CreateSpace is a service to you, so you pay them to format and print the book. Lulu charge you 20% of your sales profits and inflate their printing charges by about 35%. If your book is 150 pages long and sells for £10, your profit from Lulu will be £4.80, and from CGW your profit will be £6. You also have to pay Lulu $75 for them to list your book in the ISBN database.

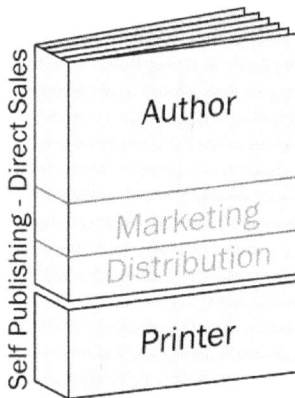

If you self publish and you want to see your book in book shops, the retailers still need a discount.

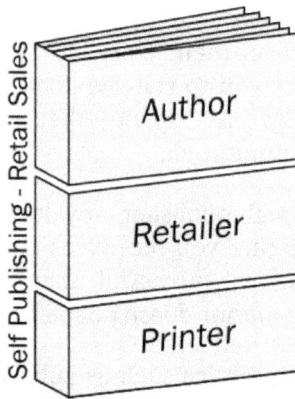

Self Publishing - Retail Sales

Author

Retailer

Printer

You have to do everything yourself to sell your book; marketing, sales, order processing, distribution, postage, which eats into your profits.

Traditional publishers seem to do all the work for you, but as you can see from their royalty figures, they're actually doing all the work for themselves. They are not really publishing 'your' book, they are licensing your copyright to create their own product. If they make you famous, you sell more books, which is very good for the publisher.

With self publishing, you actually become a publisher yourself, so you keep the full copyright, but you also have to do everything that a publisher does if you want your book to be successful.

CGW's service is somewhere between the two. We work in partnership with you, helping you to market both your book and your business.

Instead of paying you just 3% of the cover price as a royalty and using the profits to market our business, we pay you the majority of book revenue so that you can market your business, if you choose to.

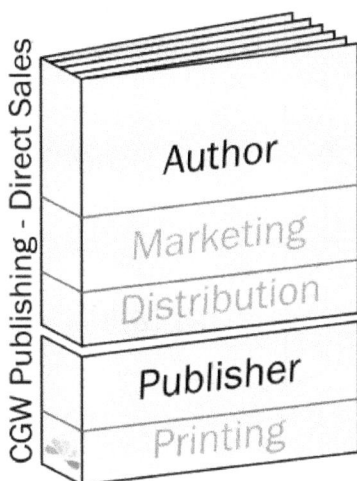

Let's say that for books that you sell direct to your clients at your seminars or other events, your overall share of the cover price is 60%.

You can either keep all of that 60% or you can spend some on marketing. You can use the book to market your business and vice versa, so you're not only marketing the book, you're including it in your overall marketing plans.

For books sold through book shops, your share of the profits from book sales might be around 40% because of the retailer's discount.

Typically, retailers would expect between 20% and 30% as a discount on the cover price.

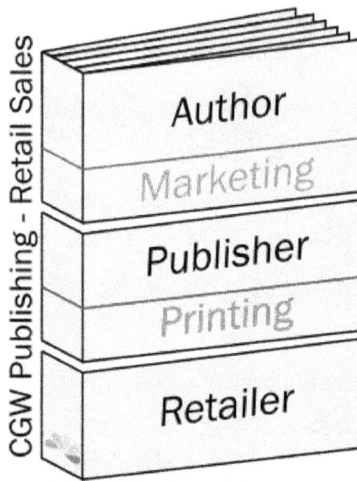

CGW Publishing - Retail Sales

Author

Marketing

Publisher

Printing

Retailer

A retailer's business is based on selling books at a profit, so we have to give them a discount in order for them to want to sell the book.

Business books rarely provide the author with a significant income in themselves. Even Stephen Covey's '7 Habits of Highly Effective People', one of the most well known and best selling business books in print today, generates income which is small compared to his income from time management products. The book has made Covey a 'household name' and that enables the Franklin Covey corporation to sell other products and services.

Our experience and expertise in helping authors to write and publish a book and then create a service business around that is based on us running a successful management consultancy for 10 years, publishing 5 books and using those books to build credibility for our business and our team.

Examples of how we support our authors include:

- Public speaking events to tell the 'story' and promote the book

- Book launch events in partnership with book shops or affiliated companies

- Training courses to teach the methods contained within the book

- Licensing the intellectual property to other trainers or consultants

- Building a database of readers for marketing the next book

- Using news media to promote the book

- Using the book as a direct sales tool

We have spent many years developing ideas and packaging those ideas as valued business services and information products.

This doesn't mean that we turn the author's idea into a book or audio CD, it means that we help the author to develop a broad yet coherent range of activities that develop a consistent brand. Every activity builds on and complements the others as the author's service business grows from a solid and stable foundation.

The author's personality is central to their brand. Too many people try to hide behind a 'corporate' image and are reluctant to take the credit for their own work, mainly because they don't believe that they have credibility.

By aligning the author's different activities so that they complement each other, the author gains the credibility that they seek and the whole brand and business grow stronger and faster.

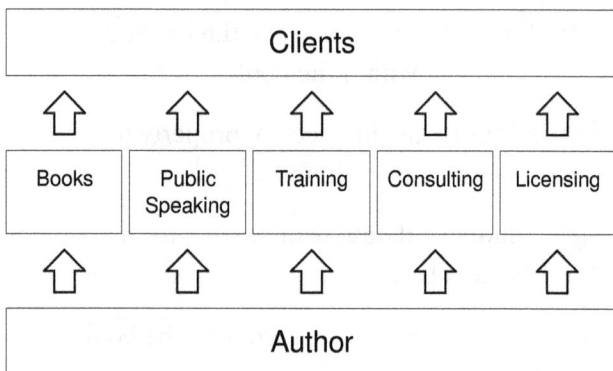

Clients

⇧   ⇧   ⇧   ⇧   ⇧

Books	Public Speaking	Training	Consulting	Licensing

⇧   ⇧   ⇧   ⇧   ⇧

Author

If you have a book inside you, we don't just help you to get it out, we help you to turn it into a successful business.

From Writer to Author

"Everyone has a book inside them"

But how did it get there?

And more importantly, how do you get it out?

At CGW Publishing, our job is to get your unique ideas and knowledge into print; whether that helps you to share your creativity and experiences or grow a successful service business.

Writing is something that we can easily take for granted; we write shopping lists and notes every day. But how many people can say that they have written a book? Almost everyone writes, but how many people can say that they are an author?

The answer is that, whilst many people say that they have always wanted to write a book, very few do.

We can help you to get your thoughts down on paper and turn them into something tangible that you can proudly share with friends, colleagues and clients.

How your book got into you is through a lifetime of unique experiences.

How to get it out?

By contacting CGW Publishing at:

mail@cgwpublishing.com

www.cgwpublishing.com

Appendix

You can place an appendix at the end of your book if you want to include information which is important but which would break the flow of the main text.

You might include reference information, further reading, a glossary of terms, some information about the author, case studies, lists of web sites, information about your other products and services and so on.

The other way that you can add information that you don't want to put in a sentence is with a footnote[3].

---

3 A footnote appears at the bottom of the page, containing information that you don't want to put in the middle of your main text because it would break the flow.

Glossary of Publishing Terms

Advance   A payment of royalties made by the publisher to the author in advance of book sales instead of after book sales.

Agent   A representative who acts on the author's behalf to find a publisher and negotiate publishing contracts.

Author   The person's name which appears on the front of the book. The author may have written the book, or they or their publisher may have engaged a 'ghost writer' to do the actual writing work.

Book   The physical product of the publishing process.

Case Bound   Another name for 'hard back' binding.

Contract   A legally binding agreement between two or more parties which sets out rights and obligations, scope and term. In other words, what one person gives the other, what they get in return, covering what activities or markets and for how long.

You'll find an example contract further on in the Appendix.

Contributor   Someone who has input to a book, for example an illustrator or contributing author. A contributor is usually listed in the book's official data record, unless they are a hired 'ghost writer'.

Copy   1. A single physical book, i.e. a copy of a book.

2. Text, usually on a web page or in a newspaper or magazine.

Copyright   Every unique piece of writing is recognised as the work of its author who has sole rights to produce copies of his or her work. Copyright is the legal recognition of an author's right to his or her creative work.

Copy Writer   Nothing to do with copyright, a copywriter is someone who writes text for magazines, product packaging, web sites and so on. This general text is called 'copy', not to be confused with a copy of a book.

Creative Commons   A form of copyright licence where the author grants a licence for anyone to freely copy and distribute their work. This is usually restricted to non-commercial applications.

Deal   A more informal name for a contract.

Distributor   A company that sits between the printer or publisher and the wholesaler. They handle distribution of book orders to either retailers or to other specialist wholesalers, such as those dealing in academic text books. A distributor might also handle imports of books into a specific country.

The terms 'distributor' and 'wholesaler' are often used interchangeably.

With Print On Demand, the printer usually acts as the distributor.

Editing   A service offered by publishers and independent editors to check and modify text for overall flow and readability.

Ghost writer Someone who does the actual writing of a book, even though the author credit will go to someone else. The majority of celebrity autobiographies are written by ghost writers. Ghost writers generally receive no royalties from book sales.

Imprint   The Imprint for a book is usually the publisher's name, however some publishers have different Imprints for different product ranges. An imprint is like a manufacturer's brand name for a product, so one manufacturer might have different brands for products sold in different markets or to different target audiences.

ISBN   International System for Book Numbering. Every book sold anywhere in the world through the normal distribution methods needs to be identified with a unique ISBN number.

Jacket   The loose printed paper cover that is often used to make hard back or case bound books look more attractive.

Literary agent   See 'Agent'.

Litho   Short for 'offset lithographic', a method of printing using metal plates which place ink onto the paper via a rubber 'offset' roller. Because of the high cost in setting up the printing plates, lithographic printing is used for large print runs, typically in the tens of thousands.

Manuscript	The plain text of the book as written by the author. It contains none of the page formatting required for printing as a book.
Margin	1. The gap between printed text and the edge of the paper.
	2. The profit made when buying something and then selling it at a higher price.
Offset	Another name for litho printing.
Pen Name	A pen name, pseudonym or nom de plume is a name chosen by an author who doesn't want to write under their own name, perhaps to write on a subject that is different from what they are normally known for, or to avoid publicity.
Perfect Bound	Another name for 'paper back' binding.
PP	Printed Pages, the number of pages in a book. Sometimes the actual number of pages in a book can be higher than the number of printed pages because the book is printed in blocks of pages which are sewn together in groups. This is why you will sometimes find a few blank pages at the end of a book.

PPC   Printed Paper Case, another name for a hardback book that has a full colour, printed cover.

Print on Demand   A method of book printing where an electronic copy of the book is kept on computer for printing only when an order is placed for the book.

Proof   A copy of a book which is produced to check for mistakes in either the original text or the printing process.

Proof reading   A service offered by publishers and independent proof readers to check text for mistakes. Computer spell checkers have difficulty correcting words which are spelt correctly even though them are nut the write ward for the sentence.

Publisher   A company that takes an author's 'manuscript' and turns it into a 'title' or printed book.

Publishing house   A company that publishes books and other information products. Usually used to describe the large, traditional publishers.

Retailer   A company which sells books. An online book shop such as Amazon works in exactly the same way as a High Street book shop.

Royalty   A payment made from a publisher to an author in return for the author granting a copyright licence to the publisher.

Short run   A print run of a small number of books. The cost per printed copy is high because the set up costs are spread across fewer copies.

Signing   An important marketing tool, a book signing is an event, normally organised in partnership with a large book shop, where the author might give a talk, read some of his or her book and then sell signed copies. The most important aspect of the signing is not book sales on the day itself but the opportunity to create marketing activity around it, for example in the local press and radio.

Supply chain   The network of different companies that are required to publish, print, distribute and sell a book. A particular supply chain can be seen by following the path of a single book from source to consumer.

Title	Another name for 'book', the word 'title' is more commonly used in the publishing and book retailing world. A consumer would normally use the word 'title' to refer to the name of a book (the title of the book), whereas a publisher or retailer would use 'title' to refer to the book itself (the title IS the book).
Title page	The first page of a book, showing the book's title, author, publisher and year of publishing.
Title page verso	The second page of a book, showing information about the book including the publisher's details, ISBN number and a copyright notice.
Wholesaler	A company that buys books in bulk and sells them on to retailers.

News Value

Here are the results from our research into the relative value of people who broadcast news on Twitter, measured in Frys.

One Fry is equivalent to the relative value of Stephen Fry's news according to his 'Followers' and 'Following' figures on 16th July 2010. In raw terms, Stephen Fry creates just over 30 times more news than he consumes.

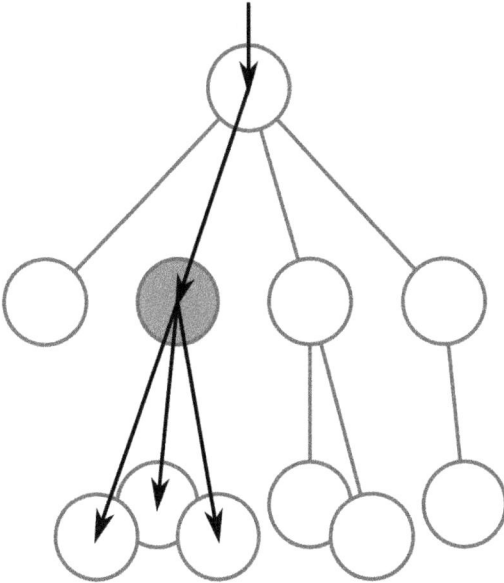

As you can see, having more followers means that the person accelerates and increases the flow of information. Fewer followers means that the person hinders the flow of information. Therefore, what we have is a way to directly measure a person's value to an information network.

You can see an important point about the popularity of business authors here; the highest selling living business author, Stephen Covey (225 Frys), is only slightly more interesting than Cheryl Cole (216 Frys), a British singer turned variety act judge, while self styled Internet marketing guru Joe Vitale, who of all people should really have mastered social media marketing, measures in at less than a tenth of a Fry. Having said that, Joe is still three times more interesting than another Internet 'guru' who claims to have lectured at Harvard Business School on the subject of marketing a business through social media channels. She scores just 30 MilliFrys.

Note that the scale on the chart on the next page is logarithmic, so each vertical line represents a value ten times greater than the one before it.

All Fry ratings were measured on 16th July 2010.

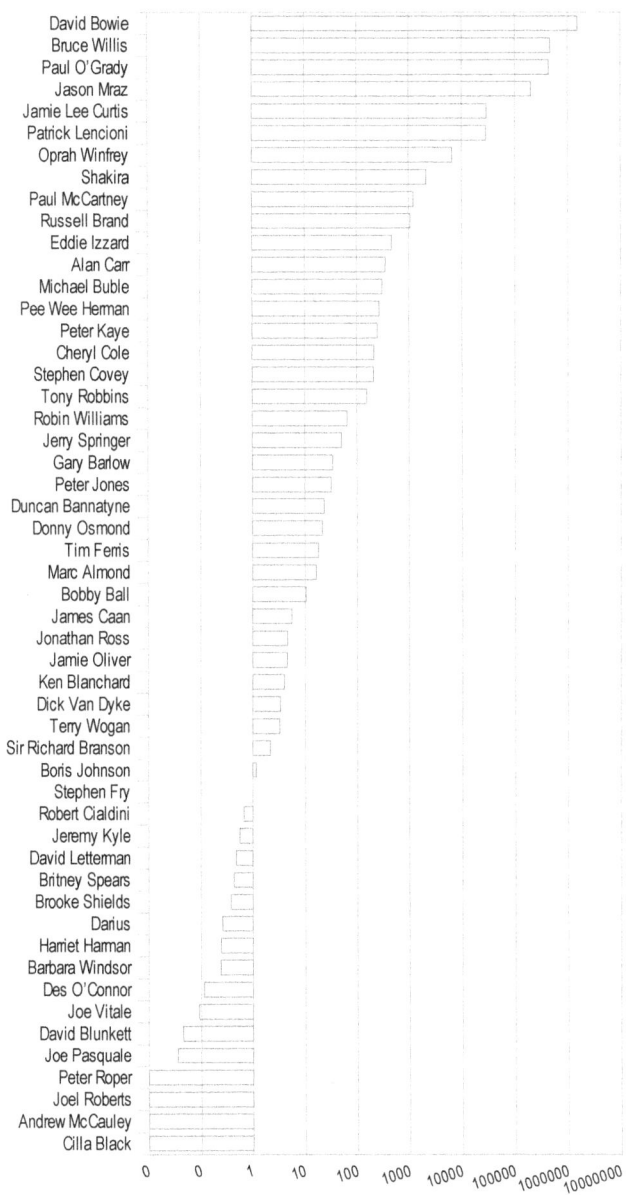

	0	0	1	10	100	1000	10000	100000	1000000	10000000

David Bowie
Bruce Willis
Paul O'Grady
Jason Mraz
Jamie Lee Curtis
Patrick Lencioni
Oprah Winfrey
Shakira
Paul McCartney
Russell Brand
Eddie Izzard
Alan Carr
Michael Buble
Pee Wee Herman
Peter Kaye
Cheryl Cole
Stephen Covey
Tony Robbins
Robin Williams
Jerry Springer
Gary Barlow
Peter Jones
Duncan Bannatyne
Donny Osmond
Tim Ferris
Marc Almond
Bobby Ball
James Caan
Jonathan Ross
Jamie Oliver
Ken Blanchard
Dick Van Dyke
Terry Wogan
Sir Richard Branson
Boris Johnson
Stephen Fry
Robert Cialdini
Jeremy Kyle
David Letterman
Britney Spears
Brooke Shields
Darius
Harriet Harman
Barbara Windsor
Des O'Connor
Joe Vitale
David Blunkett
Joe Pasquale
Peter Roper
Joel Roberts
Andrew McCauley
Cilla Black

Example Publishing Contract

Publishing Agreement

made between

Revelation Consulting Ltd trading as CGW Publishing

and

[Author's Name]

For and on behalf of the Publisher:	For and on behalf of the Author:
[Publisher's Name]	[Author's Name]
_____	_____
[Date]	[Date]

Contract reference:

CGWxxx97809565358xx

'WorkingTitle'

1 General

1.1 In these terms and conditions ("the Conditions") and in all contracts to which these Conditions apply the following words and expressions shall have the following meanings:

1.1.1 "Publishing Agreement" means this Contract and the Contract Details;

1.1.2 "the Author" means the person or company named in the Contract Details for whom the Publisher has agreed to provide the Professional Services in accordance with these Conditions;

1.1.3 "the Publisher" means CGW Publishing, a trading name of Revelation Consulting Limited. Registered in England and Wales, number 6984624. Registered office: 106 Park Road, Rugby, Warwickshire, CV21 9QX. Postal address: CGW Publishing, B1502, PO Box 15113, Birmingham, B2 2NJ, UK;

1.1.4 "the Printer" means the company selected by the Publisher for printing of books or other products covered by this Publishing Agreement;

1.1.5 "Affiliates" means owners, shareholders, officers, directors, employees, parents, subsidiaries, affiliated companies, licensees, distributors, wholesalers, retailers, suppliers, advertisers, marketers, publishers, printers, consultants, newspaper and magazine publishers, Internet service providers, lawyers, and accountants and any other person or entity to whom the Publisher extends its license or warranties to in connection with the production, dissemination, transmission, promotion, publication, or distribution of the Work or the exercise of any rights therein or derived there from;

1.1.6   "Professional Service" means professional services including but not limited to publishing, editing, proof reading, writing, ghost writing, training, facilitation, coaching, mentoring, public speaking or consultancy to be provided by the Publisher as set out in the Contract Details;

1.1.7   "Work" means the book, manuscript, audio recording, video recording or other intellectual property whose copyright is owned by the Author;

1.1.8   "Title" means the Author's Work published by the Publisher;

1.1.9   "Contract Details" means the sheet detailing inter alia the Author and the Professional Services to which these Conditions apply;

1.1.10   "Contract" means the contract between the Author and the Publisher for the provision of the Professional Services;

1.2   The headings in these Conditions are for convenience only and shall not affect their interpretation.

1.3   References to the singular shall be deemed where appropriate to include the plural and references to the masculine gender where appropriate shall be deemed to include the female gender.

1.4   These Conditions (together with the terms set out in the Contract Details in respect of each Contract) constitute the entire agreement between the parties, supersede any previous agreement or understanding and may not be varied except in writing between the parties. For the avoidance of doubt no representation or statement made by the Publisher prior to the date of a Contract shall be binding on the Publisher.

2   Professional Services

2.1   The Publisher shall provide the Professional Services for the Author in accordance with the Contract Details and subject to these Conditions.

2.2   The content of any work delivered shall, subject to variation as agreed by the parties, be determined by the Author subject to such content remaining within the agreed goals and framework of the Professional Service.

3   Charges

3.1   The Author shall pay the Publisher's Charges and any additional or other sums and expenses as agreed by the parties.

3.2   The Publisher shall be entitled to invoice the Author for the Professional Services that have been provided and for the Expenses.

3.3   If payment is not made by the Author to the Publisher on the due date, the Publisher shall be entitled, without limiting any other rights it may have, to charge interest on the outstanding amount (both before and after any judgement) at the rate of 11 per cent above the base rate of HSBC bank from the due date until the outstanding amount is paid in full.

4   Termination

4.1   The Publisher may (without limiting any other remedy) at any time terminate a Contract with immediate effect by giving written notice to the Author if any payment due to the Publisher is outstanding from the Author for more than 14 days.

5   Limitation of Liability

5.1   Subject to death or personal injury caused by the Publisher's negligence, the Publisher shall have no liability to the Author for any loss, damage, costs, expenses or other claims for compensation arising from or relating to the provision of the Professional Services.

5.2 The Author is responsible for any action taken on the advice or guidance provided by the Publisher as part of the provision of the Professional Services.

5.3 No warranty is implied by the Publisher for any advice given to the Author.

6 Confidentiality

6.1 All material or other information provided by either the Publisher or the Author which is so designated by either party or which either party might reasonably expect the other party would regard as confidential shall at any time before or after the termination of the Contract be kept confidential by both the Publisher and the Author and shall not be divulged to any person, but the foregoing shall not apply to any document or other materials, data or other information which are public knowledge at the time when they are so provided by either party, and shall cease to apply if at any future time they become public knowledge through no fault of the other party.

7 License to Publish

7.1 The Author grants to the Publisher the license to publish, store, use, transmit, distribute and sell his/her Work in print and electronic form according the the license terms set out in the Contract Details.

8   Term

8.1   The license for the Work shall extend for three (3) years after the Work's first release date. The license will automatically be renewed for consecutive one (1) year terms if neither party gives at least thirty (30) days advance written notice transmitted via electronic or standard mail prior to the end of the current term.

9   Royalty Payments

9.1   On all sales of the Work, the Publisher will pay the Author a royalty as set out in the Contract Details.

9.2   The Publisher shall pay the Author all royalties earned, on a monthly basis, within thirty (30) days of the end of each month in which the Author earned a royalty.

9.3   Costs are correct at the date of contract signature and are subject to variation.

9.4   Any changes in the Printer's charges will be notified by the Publisher to the Author.

9.5   The monthly sales report will be used as the only accurate record of costs and royalty payments due, because the Printer's handling and shipping charges will vary with the number of copies sold.

9.6   The Author may sell the Title for less than the cover price at the Author's discretion.

9.7   The Title may not be sold for more than the cover price.

9.8   If the Author wishes to change the cover price, the Publisher will update the ISBN records and amend the cover. The Printer may charge an amendment fee which will be payable by the Author.

9.9   The Author's royalty payment will be calculated as follows; the sale price of the book minus the Printer's charges, minus any retailer discount, minus any handling and shipping charges, minus the Publisher's Charges.

10   Publication Format

10.1   The Publisher and the Author will mutually agree on the Work's retail price and format.

10.2   The Publisher will source a Printer and any other necessary suppliers who are able to produce the Title in the agreed format most cost effectively..

11   ISBN management

11.1   The Publisher will allocate an ISBN number to the Title.

11.2   The Publisher will manage the Title's data record with the ISBN agency.

12   Publishing Expenses

12.1   Where the Printer charges a title set up fee, the Publisher will charge that fee to the Author.

12.2   Where the Printer charges a title maintenance fee, the Publisher will charge that fee to the Author. The Publisher may choose to deduct the title maintenance fee from any future royalty payments due the Author.

12.3   Where the Printer charges handling and shipping fees, the Publisher will charge those fees to the Author.

12.4   Where the Printer charges a fee for making alterations to the Title once it is set up, the Publisher will charge those fees to the Author.

13   Author Warranties

13.1   The Author represents and warrants the following to the Publisher:

13.1.1   The Author is the sole owner of the Work (this includes manuscript, pictures, images, drawings and any other materials submitted to the Publisher) and has the full power, authority and right to enter into this Publishing Agreement;

13.1.2   This Agreement does not conflict with any other contracts, understandings, or arrangements between the Author and any other person or entity;

13.1.3 The Work is not in the public domain and is entirely original except for portions thereof for which legally effective written licenses or permissions have been secured where necessary;

13.1.4 The Work as submitted, and its publication by the Publisher, do not and will not violate or infringe upon any personal or proprietary rights, including without limitation copyrights, trademark rights, trade secret rights, contract rights, privacy rights, or publicity rights of any other persons and entities;

13.1.5 The Work and all rights therein are free of liens, claims, interests or rights in others of any kind;

13.1.6 The Publisher shall not have any legal responsibility for the Author's Work;

13.1.7 The Work is not defamatory or obscene, or in any other way illegal; and any recipes, formulae, instructions, or recommendations contained in the Work are not and will not be injurious to any reader, user, or third person;

13.1.8 All information submitted to the Publisher is entirely accurate to the best knowledge of the Author.

14 Indemnification

14.1 The Author agrees to fully indemnify, defend and hold harmless the Publisher and its Affiliates from and against any losses, lost profits, damages, liabilities, judgements, awards, decrees, settlements, or expenses (including without limitation, reasonable legal fees and court costs) arising from, connected with, or by reason of any breach or alleged breach of any of the representations and warranties set forth above.

14.2 The Author shall not be liable for any matter inserted in the Work by the Publisher or its licensees.

14.3 All warranties and indemnifications made by the Author herein shall survive termination of this Publishing Agreement or any license hereunder.

15 Copyright Infringement

15.1 The Publisher shall have the right to commence action for copyright infringement based on the rights granted hereunder.

16 General

16.1 Any notice or communication required or permitted to be given under these Conditions shall be in writing and shall be deemed to be duly given if left at or sent by post to the registered address or principal place of business of the other party or such other address as may at the relevant time have been notified pursuant to this provision to the party giving the notice and if sent by post shall be deemed to be received three days after posting.

16.2   Neither party shall be liable to the other for any delay in or failure to perform its obligations (other than payment) as a result of any causes beyond its reasonable control.

16.3   The Publisher may substitute consulting staff in the case of unavoidable circumstances which prevent any member of staff delivering the Program.

16.4   No failure or delay by either party in exercising any of its rights under the Contract shall be deemed to be a waiver of that right, and no waiver by either party of any breach of the Contract by the other shall be considered as a waiver of any subsequent breach of the same or any other provision.

16.5   These Conditions shall in all respects be construed and take effect in accordance with English Law and the parties agree to submit to the non-exclusive jurisdiction of the English courts.

17   Contract Details

17.1   Description of Professional Service provided

17.1.1   The Author wishes the Publisher to publish the Author's Work.

17.1.2   The Publisher's role is to take the Author's original manuscript and turn that manuscript into a published book (the Title).

17.1.3   A traditional publisher would license the Author's copyright and then market the book, paying the author a small royalty for the use of the Author's copyright.

17.1.4   CGW Publishing licenses the Author's copyright and allows the Author to market the book and their business, therefore the royalty payment is significantly higher in recognition of the Author's direct marketing activities. CGW Publishing supports the Author with sales and marketing advice.

17.1.5   The Publisher's charge covers the sourcing of the Printer and other suppliers, Title management, sales report management, occasional marketing advice provided to the Author, submission of the Title and any revisions to the Printer, maintenance of book data supplied to retailers and handling of enquiries from retailers.

17.2   Publisher

17.2.1   CGW Publishing

17.3   Imprint

17.3.1   CGW

17.4   Author

17.4.1   [Author's name]

17.5   Author's contact details

17.5.1   [Author's name]

17.6   Other named contributors

17.6.1   [Contributors' name]

17.7   Title

17.7.1   [Title of book]

17.8   ISBN

17.8.1   978-0-9565358-x-x

17.9   Format

17.9.1   Printed: Perfect bound

                       Full colour cover

                       White paper inner

                       Black text

                       6" x 9"

                       300pp

                       60,000 words

17.9.2   Electronic: 6" x 9" PDF

Amazon Kindle

iBooks epub

Microsoft Reader

17.9.3   Audio: Audio CD

mp3 download

17.10   Cover price

17.10.1 £ price for UK market

17.10.2 € price for Europe market

17.10.3 $ price for USA market

17.11   Printer

17.11.1 The book will be printed and distributed by Lightning Source.

17.11.2 Lightning Source print in the UK, USA and Australia for local distribution to different territories.

17.11.3 CGW Publishing reserve the right to change suppliers if this is in the Author's best interests.

17.12   License Scope

17.12.1 Exclusive

17.13   Territory

17.13.1 All territories

17.14   Languages

17.14.1 All languages

17.15   Distribution

17.15.1 Printer to supply direct to wholesale and retail for worldwide distribution.

17.15.2 Copies available to Author for direct sales and distributions.

17.16   Marketing

17.16.1 Author is responsible for marketing the Work.

17.16.2 Publisher to provide marketing advice as required by Author.

17.17   Publisher's charges

17.17.1 The Publisher will retain the greater of 15% of the cover price or £1 per copy from the profits of sales made direct from the Printer or through the Publisher.

17.17.2 The Publisher will charge the Author the greater of 15% of the cover price or £1 on book orders supplied direct to the Author.

17.17.3 The Publisher will charge the Author £xxxx for the proof reading and editing of the manuscript and the creation of a book cover and text file ready for upload to the Printer.

17.17.4 The Publisher will charge the Author other Expenses as set out in this Publishing Agreement.

17.18   Sales routes, ordering and payments

17.18.1 There are two main sales routes for the Title, as follows:

17.18.2 Publisher Sales:

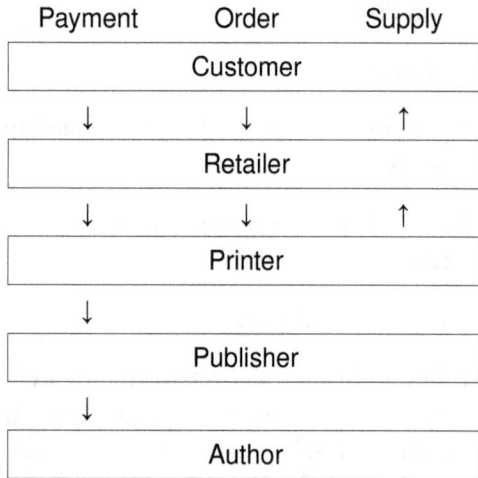

Payment	Order	Supply
Customer		
↓	↓	↑
Retailer		
↓	↓	↑
Printer		
↓		
Publisher		
↓		
Author		

17.18.3 Orders are placed and fulfilled directly between the retailer and Printer. The Printer sends the Publisher a monthly sales report and payment, and the Publisher sends a monthly sales report and payment to the Author.

17.18.4 Author Sales:

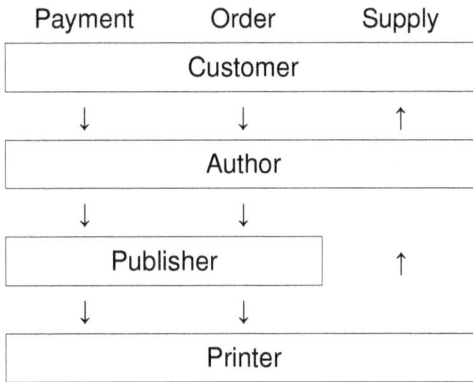

Payment	Order	Supply

Customer

| ↓ | ↓ | ↑ |

Author

| ↓ | ↓ |

| Publisher | ↑ |

| ↓ | ↓ |

Printer

17.18.5 The Author orders a quantity of books from the Publisher and sells them through their own sales channels, including retailers, the Author's website and at Author events. The Author pays the Publisher who in turn pays the Printer.

17.19   Reporting:

17.19.1 Sales reports will be provided to the Author at the end of every month for Publisher Sales

17.19.2 Sales reports will commence at the end of the first month that Publisher Sales occur.

17.19.3 No sales reports will be provided for Author Sales.

17.20   Example prices, charges and royalties

17.20.1 The table below shows indicative charges and payments for the Title.

Cover price of the Title:		£
Printer's charges for printing the Title, per copy:		£
Printer's typical charges for handling and shipping orders, per copy:		£
Publisher's charge per copy:		£
Retailer's percentage discount on cover price:	20%	£
Royalty payable per copy for orders fulfilled by the Publisher or Printer:		£
Percentage royalty, approximate:		%
Percentage royalty that would be paid by a traditional publisher, approximate:		3%
Cost per copy supplied direct to the Author:		£

Font examples

Garamond is a good choice for printed text at a size of 12 or 13 points.

10 My grandmother always had orangeade for us, and I loved to dunk my biscuits into it so that they fizzed and crackled. Of course, my mother said that this was quite disgusting, but the alternative, tea so strong that it would ooze from the teapot, was unthinkable to a small boy.

13 My grandmother always had orangeade for us, and I loved to dunk my biscuits into it so that they fizzed and crackled. Of course, my mother said that this was quite disgusting, but the alternative, tea so strong that it would ooze from the teapot, was unthinkable to a small boy.

16 My grandmother always had orangeade for us, and I loved to dunk my biscuits into it so that they fizzed and crackled. Of course, my mother said that this was quite disgusting, but the alternative, tea so strong that it would ooze from the teapot, was unthinkable to a small boy.

Times New Roman is a more traditional font and is also good choice for large areas of text. It is narrower than Garamond so is good when space is tight, such as in newspapers, but could be a little less readable in a book.

10   My grandmother always had orangeade for us, and I loved to dunk my biscuits into it so that they fizzed and crackled. Of course, my mother said that this was quite disgusting, but the alternative, tea so strong that it would ooze from the teapot, was unthinkable to a small boy.

12   My grandmother always had orangeade for us, and I loved to dunk my biscuits into it so that they fizzed and crackled. Of course, my mother said that this was quite disgusting, but the alternative, tea so strong that it would ooze from the teapot, was unthinkable to a small boy.

14   My grandmother always had orangeade for us, and I loved to dunk my biscuits into it so that they fizzed and crackled. Of course, my mother said that this was quite disgusting, but the alternative, tea so strong that it would ooze from the teapot, was unthinkable to a small boy.

Arial is a very popular, plain font. It is very clear, so it's very common in spreadsheets and technical documents. It is designed for print and is ideal at a size of 10 or 11 points.

10 My grandmother always had orangeade for us, and I loved to dunk my biscuits into it so that they fizzed and crackled. Of course, my mother said that this was quite disgusting, but the alternative, tea so strong that it would ooze from the teapot, was unthinkable to a small boy.

12 My grandmother always had orangeade for us, and I loved to dunk my biscuits into it so that they fizzed and crackled. Of course, my mother said that this was quite disgusting, but the alternative, tea so strong that it would ooze from the teapot, was unthinkable to a small boy.

14 My grandmother always had orangeade for us, and I loved to dunk my biscuits into it so that they fizzed and crackled. Of course, my mother said that this was quite disgusting, but the alternative, tea so strong that it would ooze from the teapot, was unthinkable to a small boy.

Comic is designed to emulate the hand written style used in comic books.

10 My grandmother always had orangeade for us, and I loved to dunk my biscuits into it so that they fizzed and crackled. Of course, my mother said that this was quite disgusting, but the alternative, tea so strong that it would ooze from the teapot, was unthinkable to a small boy.

11 My grandmother always had orangeade for us, and I loved to dunk my biscuits into it so that they fizzed and crackled. Of course, my mother said that this was quite disgusting, but the alternative, tea so strong that it would ooze from the teapot, was unthinkable to a small boy.

12 My grandmother always had orangeade for us, and I loved to dunk my biscuits into it so that they fizzed and crackled. Of course, my mother said that this was quite disgusting, but the alternative, tea so strong that it would ooze from the teapot, was unthinkable to a small boy.

Courier is a 'fixed width' font so all characters are the same width. It is designed for screen use, so that text can appear in neat columns.

8   My grandmother always had orangeade for us, and I loved to dunk my biscuits into it so that they fizzed and crackled. Of course, my mother said that this was quite disgusting, but the alternative, tea so strong that it would ooze from the teapot, was unthinkable to a small boy.

10 My grandmother always had orangeade for us, and I loved to dunk my biscuits into it so that they fizzed and crackled. Of course, my mother said that this was quite disgusting, but the alternative, tea so strong that it would ooze from the teapot, was unthinkable to a small boy.

12 My grandmother always had orangeade for us, and I loved to dunk my biscuits into it so that they fizzed and crackled. Of course, my mother said that this was quite disgusting, but the alternative, tea so strong that it would ooze from the teapot, was unthinkable to a small boy.

Tahoma ia a slightly more decorative font and can be tiring to read for large amounts of text.

10 My grandmother always had orangeade for us, and I loved to dunk my biscuits into it so that they fizzed and crackled. Of course, my mother said that this was quite disgusting, but the alternative, tea so strong that it would ooze from the teapot, was unthinkable to a small boy.

12 My grandmother always had orangeade for us, and I loved to dunk my biscuits into it so that they fizzed and crackled. Of course, my mother said that this was quite disgusting, but the alternative, tea so strong that it would ooze from the teapot, was unthinkable to a small boy.

14 My grandmother always had orangeade for us, and I loved to dunk my biscuits into it so that they fizzed and crackled. Of course, my mother said that this was quite disgusting, but the alternative, tea so strong that it would ooze from the teapot, was unthinkable to a small boy.

Verdana is a common screen font and is good choice for large areas of text on screen such as web pages. It is designed for use at small sizes which don't equate directly to the point sizes used for printed text.

7   My grandmother always had orangeade for us, and I loved to dunk my biscuits into it so that they fizzed and crackled. Of course, my mother said that this was quite disgusting, but the alternative, tea so strong that it would ooze from the teapot, was unthinkable to a small boy.

10 My grandmother always had orangeade for us, and I loved to dunk my biscuits into it so that they fizzed and crackled. Of course, my mother said that this was quite disgusting, but the alternative, tea so strong that it would ooze from the teapot, was unthinkable to a small boy.

13 My grandmother always had orangeade for us, and I loved to dunk my biscuits into it so that they fizzed and crackled. Of course, my mother said that this was quite disgusting, but the alternative, tea so strong that it would ooze from the teapot, was unthinkable to a small boy.

www.ingramcontent.com/pod-product-compliance
Lightning Source LLC
Chambersburg PA
CBHW060509030426
42337CB00015B/1808